The greyness of the new world juxtaposed with the greenery (life) of a new beginning in another sphere. What adventures await us there!

BOOKS BY THE SAME AUTHOR

Betrayal: – A Political documentary of our times (under penname Ashley Smith)

The Sands of Time: A book of poetry Vol 1

The Chalice: A book of poetry Vol 2

Growing Up: a collection of Children's stories and Pet Stories

Nostalgia: A book of poetry Vol 3

Conflagration: Documentary of a World in Turmoil

A Book of Plays

Wake Up Dead

The Raped Earth

CD format only: Available from author only

From Across the Waters: a Book of Recipes

Study Book Macro Skills –A Teacher's Guide and a Self Help Book for Post-Intermediate ESL learners

Study Book Micro Skills –A Teacher's Guide and a Self Help Book for Post-Intermediate ESL learners

WAKE UP
DEAD

A COLLECTION OF SHORT STORIES

SOPHIA Z. KOVACHEVICH

BALBOA.PRESS

A DIVISION OF HAY HOUSE

Balboa Press books may be ordered through booksellers or by contacting:

Balboa Press
A Division of Hay House
1663 Liberty Drive
Bloomington, IN 47403
www.balboapress.com.au
AU TFN: 1 800 844 925 (Toll Free inside Australia)
AU Local: 0283 107 086 (+61 2 8310 7086 from outside Australia)

Because of the dynamic nature of the Internet, any web addresses or links contained in this book may have changed since publication and may no longer be valid. The views expressed in this work are solely those of the author and do not necessarily reflect the views of the publisher, and the publisher hereby disclaims any responsibility for them.

The author of this book does not dispense medical advice or prescribe the use of any technique as a form of treatment for physical, emotional, or medical problems without the advice of a physician, either directly or indirectly. The intent of the author is only to offer information of a general nature to help you in your quest for emotional and spiritual well-being. In the event you use any of the information in this book for yourself, which is your constitutional right, the author and the publisher assume no responsibility for your actions.

Print information available on the last page.

ISBN: 978-1-5043-2365-9 (sc)
ISBN: 978-1-5043-2364-2 (e)

Balboa Press rev. date: 11/30/2020

TABLE OF CONTENTS

ILLUSTRATIONS:

Yesterday upon the stair
I met a man who wasn't there
He wasn't there again today
I wish that man would go away

Antigonish *– William Hughes Mearns*

PREFACE

The stories in this book are all based on love, hope, loyalty, honour kindness and on death. They are tragic as life itself is tragic but there is always hope. Hope of life and love and hope in a life after death, as all religions promise, are powerful tools for us. Death is not the end of life but only of life as we know it on this planet. It is inconceivable that we are the only planet in the galaxy to be populated. I am sure – as sure as I am alive now – at this moment that death is only a doorway to another plane of existence. Most of us at some point in our lives have experienced some form of déjà vu. How do you explain it? Or how can we account for the pain and suffering of saints and really good people while those that are far from good and who enjoy exploiting others, and do immoral and criminal deeds, seem to thrive, be successful? The answer is simple. Suffering is a way of atonement and preparation for the next phase of existence where we will be more mind and soul and less matter. The good suffer more on this earth because I think, they are closer to a higher state of being. It took me a lot of suffering and a long time to come to these conclusions. I would share my experiences with others in similar situations. Often I was a close protagonist of experiences in this book. But all the characters here were real people who experienced real pain and died. I would say to you death is an adventure and not to be feared. Whatever happens in the afterlife will enhance our experiences and perhaps make us better entities.

Then there is perfection. It is a boon to us that no one is perfect. Perfection is really negation. Perfection, as we regard it here on earth, is really hell because when everyone and everything is perfect there is no individuality and therefore, we become non-beings. So, we suffer in different ways to progress in different directions. Think for a second that every painting painted was perfect, how boring that would be and how it would render us inconsequential and unoriginal since whatever we painted was no better and no worse than that of another.

Writing this book was, in a way, cathartic for me. I was able to hone in, understand, clarify to myself and put down my philosophy of life. I believe in an after-life very different from this life. I believe in hope! It has helped me come to terms with my own humanity. This book is not at all what I envisaged when I began writing it. This book took me where it wanted to go.

THE CALM AND PEACE OF AN AFTER LIFE - TO A NEW LIFE IN DEATH THAT GOES ON. HOWEVER SOME MEMORIES WE RETAIN AT LEAST FOR AWHILE AS WE SORT OUT OUR EXISTENCE IN THE NEXT AND NEXT WORLDS.

Dedicated to all those who have faced gut-wrenching, soul-searing loss. Know this: There is hope in tomorrow no matter how bleak today looks.

WAKE UP DEAD

The greyness of the new world juxtaposed with the greenery (life) of a new beginning in another sphere. What adventures await us there!

PROLOGUE

*Up from the Earth's Centre through the
    Seventh Gate
I rose, and on the Throne of Saturn sate,
    And many Knots unravel'd by the Road
But not the Knot of Human Death and
    Fate.*

Edward FitzGerald-
Rubaiyat of Omar Khayyam *XXXI*

ANDY

My name is Andy Anderson. I went to sleep alive and woke up dead. Following is my short and poignant story.

I came from an upper middle class family. We had enough money to live well and travel all together. I had two sisters one older than me and one younger than me. I got along very well with both of them though better with my older sister. I felt we were twins. She was four and a half years older than me whereas my younger sister was seven years younger. The older one was Crystal and my younger sister was called Meredith.

I had a happy childhood. We - my sisters and I played very well together. We did not go to childcare. My time in Kindergarten was also good. I got along very well with the other children. Then began the school years. I did well at school and did not have any trouble with my studies. I liked learning especially literature and about animals and the natural environment.

My problems began when I was around ten years old. I could not get along with my father. I adored my mother.

My father was not a bad man but he was too rigid, too set in his ways, very egoistic and he could not stand any signs of sensitivity or weakness. I on the other hand, was very sensitive and cried quite easily. That irritated my father and made him punish me. I think he thought that that would harden me up and as he often said *make a man* of me. That is and was a wrong presumption. People cannot and do not change their basic nature. We are what we were born to be.

We kids used to say that he belonged to another age – the prehistoric age with all his old –fashioned ideas - no freedom for the kids, how a man has to always to have a stiff upper lip and should appear to be insensitive and so on. My poor, darling mum! We could never understand what she had ever seen in him.

My father drank too much and we thought that is what made him so nasty. We kids learned early to stay out of sight and away from him when he was drinking which was a lot of the time. He didn't work because everything was taken care of by the business managers. Still there were the good times especially when he travelled alone overseas and we had mum to ourselves. Those were always great times. We looked forward to them.

My mother on the other hand was perfect. She was kind, loving sensitive. She was the best mother any child could ever have. We were lucky children to have had her and her love. She tried to shield me as much as possible from my father's wrath but rarely succeeded. My father got madder when she tried to protect me and so she stopped and moved away when there was a confrontation between my father and me. My sister Crystal stepped in. She was fearless and often challenged my father. But more of that later.

As a family I suppose we were an average family. All families go through troubled times and we were no exception. I cannot say I was very happy except for the times my father was away but I was more or less contented. We were not billionaires nor were we poor. I suppose you could say we belonged to the upper middle class. We had enough to satisfy all what we wanted.

Now, about my unnerving experience:

One second I was alive and in my bed, the next second I was in a totally alien and unfamiliar landscape. The only colour tone was grey. Everything about and around me was grey. There was an eerie silence all around. No one spoke but I suppose we were able to communicate through thought waves. No one seemed to want to communicate, including me.

With me, when I wakened, I felt disoriented and lost even though there were other souls also looking lost. This topic is taboo – to talk to the living about the dead as I mentioned before. What I can say is that we pay our debts before moving on. We pay for our sins. And the more innocent you are, the faster you move to the next stage where it is good – not that it is bad here but just alien at first. I wonder if this is to prepare us for the next stop. Or if there is even another stop!!! Time will disclose all, though here I don't think we can feel time the same way as I used to feel it before. I can't as yet feel time at all — just this eerie greyness and silence.

All around me the others look lost so I must be looking lost too but to tell you the truth I think it is rather nice not to hear anything. There is a strange, deep silence around us. I wonder if I look like the others! You can't really make out anyone's shape or size or features. Everyone and everything here is colourless but you just know when it is another soul close by and when it is not. I think I am happy that I am here and won't ever have to be scolded or punished again.

We who are here came here in various ways but no one came here by fluke. We were all meant to be **here today**. I feel no pain or discomfort but some here do. Perhaps it's because they have not yet accepted their situation and are still hankering for the other world. I don't know how I know but I do. We don't talk in words as you know them but we do communicate. For example when I woke up and found myself here I felt the presences around me welcoming and comforting me in I don't know which language but in a way I could understand them perfectly. I'm rather excited to be here.

THE BEGINNING

In my beginning was my end, and in my end may be a new beginning.

Sophia Z Kovachevich

Ah, fill the Cup: - what boots it to repeat
How Time is slipping underneath our
Feet:
Unborn TO-MORROW and dead YESTERDAY
Why fret about them if TO-DAY be sweet!

Edward FitzGerald-
Rubaiyat of Omar Khayyam XXXVII

MRS ANDERSON

My beautiful boy! He is too good for this cruel world. He is a very sensitive soul. I can't protect him. When I intervene, things get worse so it's best I keep out of the way. George says I baby him too much and will make him into a namby-pamby. This world is a very harsh place and I often worry as to how he's going to manage.

It's good that he has two sisters who adore him and look out for him, especially the older one. Crystal is sensitive but tough. She easily holds her own with her father. I think her father respects her for her strength of character. I also think he is disappointed in his only son, which is wrong. We are all different and that difference is what makes the world a more interesting place. Meredith is still only a child but she follows where Crystal leads - always.

Andy is very intelligent and up and doing. What unravels him is his sensitivity. And it is this that causes his father to pick on him, criticise him and sometimes even raise his hands on my poor baby. But I cannot report that. It will make matters worse and bring shame on the family. I hope things change soon for the better. A good thing is that Andy too follows Crystal and looks to her for comfort and protection from my husband, his father.

My husband is not a bad man. He is just difficult, insensitive and too demanding. I know he loves all the children but he has no patience at all with Andy and his inability to please him and be the man his father wants him to be. He also does not know how to show his love for the children to them. Meredith is just a child but she sees her father's reaction to Andy and she too avoids him as much as she can. She won't go near her father without Crystal holding her hand.

I don't worry about Crystal. She can always hold her own. She is a big help to me in many ways not just with Andy and Meredith.

The past four – five years have been more difficult than usual. George is my husband but he has started to push Andy to man up so to speak, as it were, and poor darling child that is alien to his nature. He just cannot do it. For example, take the incident with the gun. George wants to teach Andy to hunt. Andy hates hunting or hurting any living creature and he won't use the gun. That makes George simply incensed because he loves going hunting and the 'manly' sports, which Andy hates. Andy is happier reading or playing with his sisters or listening to music or playing on his guitar. I really don't know how to help the two of them. They are like chalk and cheese. Andy avoids George as much as possible. Perhaps it's better that way because whenever they are together there is shouting (from George) which reduces Andy to tears and makes George angrier still. What a mess it all is!

I try to teach my children what I think are the life values so how can I now tell them to ignore those values and do as their father tells them to do? I have always told my children that it is very important to be true to themselves and everything will follow from that. I have taught them to avoid even white lies as much as possible. So how am I to tell them now to betray their very instinctual responses and pretend to be what George wants them to be?

Now, to go back to the gun incident. As I said George wanted to teach Andy to shoot. Andy is a pro-life person who hates guns and all forms of violence so he refused to even touch the gun, leave alone to fire it. George lost his temper and started to shout. Andy started to cry. George lost his temper some more and slapped Andy a couple of times. Meanwhile Meredith who was watching from a distance rushed to get Crystal. I sighed in relief. Crystal came, shouldered Andy out of reach of George, picked up the gun and said for all to hear: *Watch me fire.* She aimed for a fruit on the tree and dropped it as all watched her. George's mood changed in the wink of an eye.

He forgot about Andy's refusal and started with Crystal firing at clay pigeons to see whose aim was better. Of course, George won. It would never do for anyone else to win in a competition with George. That incident, I hope, highlighted for you how little it takes for George to lose his temper with Andy and reduce him to tears.

Then there was the other gun incident when George pulled a gun on Andy – (probably to scare him and he did that too!) Andy was a mess and then again Crystal stood in front of her brother with the gun pointing at her saying not a word. George shoved the gun into a drawer and someone put it back in the locked cupboard where it was meant to be.

There were other incidents in other situations but these two stand out for me as they were the most frightening of all. It was very good that everything was resolved in a proper way. No physical harm was done but these had a deep psychological impact on all the children especially Andy.

Meredith is just a baby and so, I need not worry too much about her as yet. And she has her siblings to take care of her especially Crystal whom she follows around like a shadow. Meredith however, is not going to be as gentle as Andy. She already shows a strength that Andy does not show. At the moment she is everyone's pet.

Then there is Crystal. She is strong but very sensitive which she covers up well. She knows how to stand her ground for herself and her siblings. She is the only one who can face her father when he is in a rage. She knows how and when to speak and when to shut up. I don't really worry about her. She is my very independent child.

Things have a way of working out. I hope the future will be bright and happy for all my three children. I worry about them, especially Andy. He's too sensitive for this harsh world that we inhabit.

MEREDITH

I am Meredith Anderson. I am five years old - one-two-three-four-five. 5 fingers are 5 years. I am five-five-five. I love chocolate and candies and Max. Max is bigger than me. He is a dog. Sometimes he hides his bones with my toys and I give it to him. He likes to play with me and my dolls, especially my doll, Woolly. She is very soft. In my family there is me, mum and dad and Crystal and Andy and Max and Woolly and Jackson, my koala. We are happy now. Oh I love ice cream but mum says I can't have it in winter or when I am sick. So I don't. Dad sometimes brushes my hair but I have to stand very still. I don't like it. I like my mum or Crystal to brush my hair. Mum often tells me little stories when she does so. Crystal teaches me nursery things like *Mary had a little lamb.* Her lamb was like my Jackson. I hope I get a big doll that can walk and talk for my this birthday, and for Christmas I want a big white bear and lots and lots and lots of chocolates. Did I tell you I love chocolates! Yum!

Sometimes Mum is sad. I don't like mum to be sad so I kiss her and tell her that I love her. Andy is often sad and sometimes he cries and when I ask him why and he says not to think about that but I do. I don't want Andy to cry. I love Andy he gives me lots of piggy back rides. Dad shouts too much, I think he loves to be angry but that makes me nervous and I run away and hide. Crystal is fun. I like being with her. She makes me happy. Oh I can't talk anymore. I have to go. It is time for Woolly and Jackson to eat.

CRYSTAL

Dad really must stop this male macho thing. I think he thinks it is good - this male dominance thing coming out – this constant criticising of Andy, his shouting at him for the smallest of infractions. Sometimes he strikes, and that is unacceptable. It is wrong. Andy can't take it.

Poor, darling Mum! She is always caught in the middle and yet when she voices her displeasure at Dad's behaviour the situation worsens. Dad is too competitive, arrogant and mean. Though I must say he is very generous especially to his friends and he's also very smart. I think he is bored and so takes it out on others.

I get along okay with dad. But I love Mum much, much more. Perhaps Dad senses that we kids are more attached to Mum and so he reacts in this way. But all children are attached to their mothers when they are young.

Another good thing about Dad is that he allows us to have pets. Meredith really loves Max, the dog, the way she loves her Woolly and Jackson. Of all her toys these are her favourite ones, as much if not more, than people.

THE PASSAGE OF TIME

The Moving Finger writes; and, having
    Writ,
Moves on: nor all thy Piety nor Wit
        Shall lure it back to cancel half a Line,
Nor all thy Tears wash out a Word of it.

Edward FitzGerald---
Rubaiyat of Omar Khayyam LI

ANDY

This year I've finished Secondary school. I like computers and computer work. However, I don't like Physics and Maths. I'm glad I did quite well on both subjects. All other subjects are okay. I have begun my A Levels. Everything is different now. The workload is heavier, more homework and more responsibilities. Still it's fine.

I've made some new friends and sometimes we hang out together. We also work together when it is on group projects.

Life at home is better for two main reasons. The first is that I spend less time at home so I see less of my dad. And where that is concerned, things are about the same. I am still not comfortable around him and we still do not see eye to eye on most topics. The second reason is that my dad is travelling overseas more these days. So the house is really peaceful.

Yesterday we had a couple of tests. I think I did well on them. Now I have to wait for the results to be sure. They were easy. I must do well on my A level exams. I think I want to do my higher studies in in ornithology or palaeontology or perhaps even in computer programming. Our teachers are okay in general but I really don't care for field trips. I like working in the lab though.

I don't have any girlfriends as yet though most in my group do. I want to finish my A levels with very good grades and begin university, before I begin any relationships. And anyway I haven't yet met anyone that I am very attracted to.

Recently I read a very interesting book about Stephen Hawkins. One cannot help admiring that man – what courage! What grit!

Yesterday Shawn and Adrian offered me to do drugs with them. I refused. I'm afraid of getting hooked on it. Drugs are bad and it's better to avoid it when possible, I think! I must speak to Crystal about this. She's sure to have a lot to say about this topic. She is very much against drugs like these. Two of her friends died because of drug addiction. One of them she liked a lot and he liked her too. They were at the university together in the same class, studying the same subject. Though she doesn't talk about him, I think she cared a lot about him. His parents liked Crystal a lot and asked her to try and influence him to stop taking drugs but she once said it was by then, too late. His oesophagus and stomach lining by then were in a bad way.

I'd better get back to my studies and read up the work for tomorrow's class. I like being prepared for my classes.

CRYSTAL

I'm worried about Andy. I don't like him mixing with these boys. I don't like it that they do drugs, but if I tell him so he'll have some comforting words for me. I don't want words. I don't need to hear words. I need him to be safe.

I think it is bad when it's so easy to get your hands on these terrible drugs. Young kids are at risk. I know I'm also young but I believe that I am rather more mature than others of my age. I've always had to keep my brother's and to a lesser extent, Meredith's backs. Then I have also had to make sure Mum doesn't feel slighted by Dad's bad behaviour with everyone. Mum needs an outlet like everyone else and with Dad always underfoot, it is hard to relax. It's good that now he travels more often overseas and best of all – alone. We get Mum all to ourselves and there is such peace and calm everywhere. Everyone is relaxed and we spend all the time – except for school and homework – with her.

I have to decide very soon what I want to do with my life. I think after I finish my degree in literature I must decide what path to take or to change.

Andy is never far from my thoughts. His dark periods have become more frequent and they last longer. These breaks from Dad's presence are vital for him.

I'm glad he told me on his own about the boys. I feel it in my bones that it is just a question of time before he slips and tries something if he gets too close to these boys.

Drugs have become so easy to get. And there are so many types. As our world becomes more and more complicated and people suffer from depression and breakdowns, more and more drugs are available on the market. Then we have prescription medicine. Andy has been diagnosed with severe depression and has to take some tablets — antidepressants - to control his depression. He also takes sleeping pills. I hope he stops soon.

Still the drugs help him a lot. He is less nervous even when he is near Dad – which, by the way, is a rare occurrence.

What worries me the most is that it is a fine line that he is treading with these friends. I've heard and read about too many cases when young people tipped over the edge from controlled drug taking to to that horrible word – overdose…suicide. Too many of our youth take that slippery path and become addicted and worse. USA is believed to have the highest victims followed by Australia and then here in the UK.

The thing is *I can't talk to anyone about this*. Mum has enough to worry about without me adding to it. Moreover, I promised Andy that I would not tell a soul about the drugs his friends take and so I can't. I think I'll research this, put it on paper and see where to go from there and what to do. The problem here is that, okay--Andy will refuse 2, 3, 6 times. What happens the seventh time? And these drugs have an insidious quality of making you addicted to them leading to bigger and bigger doses. No, I must resolve this somehow. Thank God Andy trusts me enough to tell me about it. I think it's best if he mixes with a different set of friends who don't do drugs. Though it seems to me that at this age most kids, at this time try drugs – maybe due to peer pressure or the excitement of the forbidden or because those around them do it and they want to fit in.

Now I must go and see about the preparations for Meredith's birthday party.

MEREDITH

Tomorrow is my birthday. Oh what fun! I wonder what presents I'll get. I hope I have a nice party and a nice strawberry cake with my name on it. I asked mum if I could invite some friends from my group and she agreed. So it's going to be a big party

I'll wear my new blue dress. It is very pretty with matching shoes. I wanted heels but mum said I couldn't wear heels yet. That's alright. High heels are not really comfortable and you can't run or play in them.

Andy bought me a disc player and two CDs of my favourite songs. Crystal bought me a book and a bracelet. I'll wear my new bracelet today. I don't yet know what mum and dad got me. I hope it's something I like.

I think our dogs know it is my birthday. They are all around me today jumping and licking especially Max. Max is my favourite.

I wish time would pass more quickly and my party would begin. Ohhh I'm so happy and excited.

MRS ANDERSON

Meredith is such a happy child. She's got a very sunny disposition and it draws people to her. She is a proper happy little girl with a little girl's attitudes and desires.

Crystal was never so. She was and still is a very serious, oversensitive young girl. She takes responsibilities on her little shoulders that she really shouldn't have too. But I don't worry about her. She'll be okay. There is tensile strength in her.

My main worry is Andy. The older he's getting the more I worry about him. There is a sort of helplessness about him. He is too sensitive and there appears to be an unprotected air about him. The world is a harsh place and if you are helpless you become a prey. He has no protective armour about him. Yes, he no longer cries each time someone hurts him but the hurt shows clearly in his face and in his eyes. He must become tougher. At least now he seems to be happy most of the time. His relations with his father have not improved at all and there is nothing anyone can do about it. Both feel let down by the other. They are so totally unalike in every way that it is hard to believe they are father and son. George is too tough and insensitive. His first reaction to anything is to punch back, often physically. He feels his son has let him down with what he calls Andy's *namby-pamby ways*. That simple sentence shows you how little they understand each other.

I'm glad there peace at home these days. It's good that George travels so much. It makes for the smooth functioning of the house without anger, shouting and the accompanying tension. I also don't like George's drinking habits. He often gets drunk and becomes irascible and nasty. And of course then he has to pick on Andy. If Andy is not around – which is usually the case – he calls for him to light into him. Andy just stands there and the hurt shows clearly on his face. I wish he'd stand up for himself as Crystal does. She not only stands up for herself – though she seldom has clashes with George over herself. Her clashes with George are generally over Andy. It's time for Andy to really stand up to George. Then George would perhaps respect him more and perhaps get off Andy's back. George likes confrontations. George is back tomorrow. At least Meredith's party will be celebrated in peace. She is so excited.

THE AWAKENING

Awake for Morning in the bowl of Night
Has flung the Stone that puts the Stars
To Flight:
And Lo! The Hunter of the East has
Caught
The Sultan's Turret in a Noose of Light.

Edward FitzGerald-
Rubyaiyat of Omar Khayyam I

ANDY

Last night I went to a party – a party that I hadn't really wanted to go to. One of my friends was celebrating the end of the school year. There was a lot of beer and other alcoholic and non-alcoholic drinks, finger food and later on in the evening, drugs. I did not take any of the drugs. It would not do to become addicted to that. But the most beautiful thing in the whole world happened to me. I'm in love – madly, badly, totally and completely. She is what I have waited all my life for. Just looking at her was enough for me but then she came over to where I was sitting and asked me my name and what I would like to have. I lost my tongue totally and just nodded. She touched me on my right shoulder and said *Take your time.* The words were music to my ears. Is this really love? My whole world was focussed on her. I stayed at the party much longer than I had intended to.

I have no idea what I ate or drank or what I said but I left soon after she spoke to me because I wanted to savour what had happened to me. I was really over the moon. Is this love? Or is something else? I lay awake all night long going over every second from the moment I laid eyes on her. And I wondered if I would see her again or how to find out more about her.

Sleep finally came during the early hours of the morning.

When I woke up my first thought was about her. I felt even more in love – if that were possible. I worried how to find her again then wonder of wonders I *found her number in my pocket.* Her name is Sylvia – music to my ears. I wanted to call her immediately but my inner voice told me to wait till after 10 am. She might be asleep and would not be too happy to be woken up by some unknown person.

Time hung heavy on my hands. The minutes dragged on. I was desperate to speak with her and speak with her and speak with her. I had a million questions for her. She was my first and only love. The world suddenly seemed a beautiful place to be in. I felt I could take on the whole world and come out tops. Sylvia my Sylvia where are you?

Finally it was 10am and I dialled her number but before she could answer I lost my nerve and hung up. Then I called again full of trepidation and anticipation at the same time but I had to know.

Sylvia answered. I introduced myself but she said she knew who I was and she knew a lot about me that I had told her the night before. I was not aware of that. She was so easy to talk to. We agreed to meet for lunch at a restaurant we both liked.

I asked Crystal to lend me some money because I had no idea how much lunch with my dream girl would cost and I did not want to be embarrassed. Of course Crystal lent me a good amount. It is my first date. I'm nervous. What if she doesn't come? Or, if she's not interested? Or, if she already has a serious boyfriend? I'm getting more nervous by the minute. I'll speak with Crystal. She knows how to calm me down and she's knows people better than I do. If anyone can help me now, it is Crystal.

CRYSTAL

So it has happened. Andy thinks he's in love. I'm very pleased for him but at the same time I am nervous. He is emotionally, very fragile. When he loves, he loves completely. The same is with trust. He doesn't trust a lot of people but when he does it is with no holds barred. Let's not jump the gun. We'll wait and see how this pans out. It could be just a momentary thing. After all he is almost an adult and the hormones are all waking up and it is a difficult time both psychologically, emotionally and even physically. He is a late developer and so it is bound to hit him harder.

Perhaps this is the best thing that could happen to him. I hope their lunch-time date is a rip roaring success.

Meredith regards Andy as her special friend. I hope she does not get too jealous. I must speak to Andy about this. But wait – I'm perhaps jumping the gun too. It could well be a flash in the pan. I'm worried because I have never seen him so excited and fixated and happy. I'd love for him to be happy always – if that is possible. Let's wait and see how this meeting goes. I have told him not to tell her that he loves her – just yet. This meeting should be about getting to know each other better and establishing a good friendship. Relationships based on friendship are richer and more lasting than those based on only physical attraction.

SYLVIA

I don't get it. There's something about this young man that pulls at my heartstrings. This has never happened to me before. Perhaps I should not have given him my number but when he asked if he could see me again, I just could not say no. If he calls that'd be great. If not well – then it wasn't meant to be.

I'd better go and get Des ready for school.

The phone is ringing. Maybe it is him. I'd better get it. Oh! It stopped. Oh well…

It's the darned phone again. I'd better get it on the off chance it's Andy. Lovely name - strong and true.

It was Andy. We're meeting up for lunch. I can't really believe it!! What shall I wear? Something flattering but discreet, I think. Perhaps my lucky blue one or maybe the flattering red and black one – no I'll wear the understated green. No makeup. I have butterflies in my stomach. I can't quite believe it all. After all, I'm a mature person and we only met last night. I have never felt such attraction before – not even with Des' dad. Could I have fallen in love?

I hope our lunch is very successful and we get to know each other better. I'll play it by ear. No point in preparing questions and answers before-hand in my head. He seems such a lovely person, kind, gentle and a very smart young man. I wonder if Des will take to him. I hope he does. That would make things much easier for me.

How the time has flown. I must be getting along. Just one last look to make sure everything is as it should be.

I hope he recognises me. After all, he saw me in dim lights at night.

ANDY

Gosh she's here and oh so beautiful. What shall I say? Maybe she won't like me after all. But I must stop behaving like a puppy in love and pull myself together. At the worst it will be a disaster and we will both realise our mistake. Still it's worth a shot.

I have never felt this way before. I have never wanted to be with someone and for that person to like me as I want her to. I'll take Crystal's advice and be myself – not try to be someone or something different to who I really am. If it is meant to be, it will be and nothing and no one can change that.

Well, here goes!

SYLVIA

Holy Moly he looks even better in the light. But there seems to be a shadow of pain on his face. No. It's just my imagination. He looks younger than I thought he was.

Well let's get to know each other and let's take each day as it comes. I'm rather excited about this unexpected turn of events. No point in rushing anything. What will be, will be - *Que sera sera*. Let's see what life has in store for us. That's the best that we can do – the chips will fall where they will. I hope he recognises me, well yes, he's coming over.

A few months later

The passing of time following the change of seasons

ANDY

These have been the best months of my entire life. The more I see Sylvia, the more I love her. She is kind, fair and oh so beautiful. *My cup runneth over.* Most important of all she understands me and never puts me down or tries to change me. I love her.

She told me that she is divorced with a young son. That's fine by me. I've met her son Des and we have bonded well. I've also met her ex, Matthew. He's okay. And he is okay about Sylvia and me – not that he has any right to interfere but Des is his son and it could have led to a confrontation which I really hate.

Des is a good boy. I'm teaching him Monopoly. He already knows to play Ludo. Sometimes we play that. I bought him some simple jigsaw puzzles. He loves them. Later I'll get him more and more difficult ones.

Sylvia loves the cinema and we have spent some lovely times there. I like going to the cinema too. We see all kinds of films. Sometimes we take Des with us when he wants to see some cartoon films. Life is great.

Sylvia was worried that she's a bit older than me but I told her it doesn't bother me – in fact it is good. Her maturity is another positive. Not all people gain wisdom and understanding as they grow older. Point – my dad is not mature. He can't control his temper at all. He thinks the world does and should revolve around him. Of course my Sylvia is much younger but in my opinion, she is much more mature than Dad. He's eased up a lot because I think now that he travels so much he has less time to concentrate on unimportant things like yelling at me or at someone else. Even our pets look happier these days.

SYLVIA

The more I get to know Andy, the more I like him. He's not like other young men his age. He appears quite mature in many ways; and really young and defenceless in others. After a long time I feel really happy. I look forward to seeing Andy every day. I must ask Andy about Crystal. He often talks about his sisters especially Crystal. I'd like to meet her. She seems to have a lot of influence on Andy.

Time is just flying. It is almost a year since Andy and I met but it seems like it was yesterday. Des loves Andy. They have bonded really well – even better than with Matthew. Could be because Matthew has remarried and he has a little child or could be because Matthew doesn't relate very well to kids. Anyway…

Andy wants us all three of us - to go away on a holiday. He asked me where I'd like to go. I think Bath would be a nice place to go to. Des will love the beach. I'll see if we can find some rock pools and then Andy and I can show Des the sea creatures that live under rocks.

I'm happy and contented.

CRYSTAL

It was good meeting Sylvia. She is a lovely person. I can see what attracts Andy to her. She is more mature than her years. Her son is a very well behaved and quiet child. I think Sylvia offers Andy not just love and acceptance but also a safe refuge from the buffets of life. They look very good together. We must have her over more often.

Mum too likes her. Mum says she has a sweet nature and is mature for her age. Mum says having a child is probably what forced her to mature earlier. Sylvia doesn't talk much. She listens and makes pertinent points. But Mum says that she is probably quite lonely. Being a single parent must curtail her social life. I agree because whenever Andy rings, most of the time she is at home.

Like Sylvia, Andy too has a very limited social life. He has a few friends who he sees every now and again. He spends a lot of time at home, pursuing his studies and his hobbies. One good thing that came out of his meeting with Sylvia is that he has distanced himself from his drug-taking friends.

Sylva will have to meet Dad and I think it's best if I introduce her as my friend. I must speak to Andy about it. This looks like a serious relationship and it cannot be hidden from Dad forever. If we introduce her as Andy's girlfriend, I know Dad will flip and there will be long lectures and he will light into Andy about wasting time etc. etc. etc. Perhaps we'll get this over with at the coming weekend. Dad is expected to be home for a while come Wednesday. I don't want anyone to upset the fragile peace that we have at home when Dad's around. Once Dad accepts Sylvia – and I'm sure he will, we can go the next step. And if they are really serious – which we all think they are, we can tell Dad she's now Andy's girlfriend. And then the fireworks will start. Any bet on that! But maybe I'm just getting ahead of myself. It could also be a strong passing attraction. After all they are both young even though she is a bit older than Andy.

SYLVIA

I like Crystal. I'm glad we met. I can see why Andy is so attached to her. Funny Des took to her at first sight. He doesn't often do that. He is a shy child and takes his time forming new relationships. Now I've met most of the family. I only have Andy's dad to meet. That worries me. What if he says Andy can't see me because I have a son, that I'm divorced and that I'm too old for him. Andy lives at home. He can't go against his father's orders. Never mind. We'll take that stile when we come to it.

Meredith is very sweet and naughty. She is full of questions. They are a happy family from what I've seen.

Des' birthday is coming up. I hope my mum and brother can come. We'll have a small family party. I would like to invite Andy's family too. I must ask him when I see him today. I'd like my mother to meet Andy and his family but especially Andy. I hope she likes him and Andy likes her.

I think I'll get the jumping castle. All kids like that – not that there'll be a lot of kids – just a handful from Des' day-care place and Andy's little sister.

ANDY

That meeting went really well. I think they liked each other and Meredith got another person to do her bidding. Mum also seemed to like Sylvia. Things seem to be going well. I'm very happy these days. The studies are going well and I like gaining knowledge.

Tomorrow I'm going to buy an engagement ring for Sylvia. It will be a surprise for everyone. Tomorrow night I will take Sylvia out and propose after dinner. I'd like to buy her an emerald ring surrounded by diamonds. Maybe I should ask Crystal. She would know what girls like. I don't want to buy just diamonds because everyone does, but I know she likes green so a green stone it will be. I think emeralds are green.

Oh I'm so excited but at the same time a little apprehensive. What if she says no? Or if she thinks it's too soon. I couldn't bear that. I won't think about it.

I'll listen to some music and go talk to Crystal. We have always spent time together. She's not only my sister, she is also my closest friend. Meredith is too young but she is a pet. We all spoil her.

A few years later

THE COMPLICATION

Tomorrow, and tomorrow, and tomorrow,
Creeps in this petty pace from day to day,
To the last syllable of recorded time;
And all our yesterdays have lighted fools
The way to dusty death. Out, out, brief candle!
Life's but a walking shadow, a poor player,
That struts and frets his hour upon the stage,
And then is heard no more.

William Shakespeare –
Macbeth ACT V; SCENE V

ANDY

I asked Crystal to come with me to get a girl's perspective on it. We bought a very pretty emerald ring surrounded by diamonds. I would give my all for Sylvia. When we finished I rang and settled with Sylvia to go out for dinner. I did tell her it was a very special occasion. I didn't tell her why. I want to see the surprise on her face. She is such a lovely person. I never thought I'd meet someone like her. She seems to not only understand me but also my moods. I know I can sometimes be over sensitive and difficult. Like my sister, she knows how to make me feel better. I hope all goes very well!

SYLVIA

I wonder what Andy has up his sleeve. He said very special. Could he be planning to propose? Of course I'll say YES! YES! YES! But perhaps it's something much more mundane like going to the cinema or making some plans for the Christmas season. I can't do anything much more than wait and see. He's asked me to wear something green. That is a very strange request. He's never asked me such a weird thing before. I'll wear my green and black evening dress and put my hair up. No jewellery. The dress is enough of a statement. I wonder if he's bringing some guests with him and that's why he asked to dress up.

Tonight after dinner I'll tell Andy I want to invite his family for Des' birthday especially because my mother and brother will certainly come. My mum dotes on Des. After all, he's the only grandchild she has.

Andy and I have been together for a while and in this time our relationship has grown. It often feels like I've known him forever. I love everything about him – the strengths and the weaknesses. I hope it is the same for him. Actually it feels as if he does. And my darling baby also loves him. He gets on better with Andy than with his father. Oh I must tell Andy that Matthew and his wife are expecting another baby probably in May or June.

ANDY

Last night was just perfect. I proposed after dinner and Sylvia happily accepted. I am so happy that I have no words to express it. Sylvia did suggest that we wait until after I finish my studies before getting married. I'm doing my Bachelor's Degree in Computer Technology. But I don't want to wait. We can get married next year and I'll move in to her flat and we'll share the rent. I'll get a part-time job till I finish Uni. Sylvia suggested we sleep on it a little.

When I came back after dinner, I was too happy and excited to sleep and went to see Crystal and Mum. They are both happy for me but both think we should wait like Sylvia also suggested. I told them that. Soon afterwards, Mum went to bed but Crystal and I talked late into the night. I don't remember all what we talked about. We opened a bottle of champagne to celebrate.

Today I could not concentrate on the lecture at all but kept doodling Sylvia's name all over my notes. I am the luckiest and happiest person in the world.

Meredith said that Sylvia called and invited all of us to her son's birthday party. Meredith is very pleased. She loves parties.

MRS. ANDERSON

Andy is engaged. We've got to have them over for a celebratory dinner. George says he won't be back till next month. I think we'll go ahead anyway and have another dinner when George returns. I wonder how he'll take it. One can't always tell with George how he'll react to any unexpected situation. It will also depend on the success or not of his trip and on his mood. There is also the fact that George always likes to be the centre of attention. He hates to share the limelight and it will be Andy's day and Andy's limelight. Oh I do hope all goes well.

Now we have been invited to Desmond's birthday. I think we'll give cash. Crystal says she will buy a separate present since she works. Meredith – as usual is very excited at going to a party. And now she wants to be Sylvia's flower girl.

I'm rather worried at how George's going to react.

It has been very good seeing Andy so happy, contented and focussed on his studies in spite of everything else. Since knowing Sylvia, he has really matured a lot. His depressive periods have also become less. She has really been a very good influence on him.

SYLVIA

I'm over the moon with joy. I wasn't sure about the proposal. The ring is beautiful and oh so elegant. Andy wants to get married as soon as possible but I still think he should finish Uni. first and then look for a job. I want our lives to be as smooth as possible. If he studies and works, his studies will suffer and he will be tired. I saw that happen with my first marriage and I don't want a repetition. Often the couple start blaming each other and love sours. So I will try and convince Andy to wait. Meanwhile I have to get the room ready for my mum. Jack can sleep on the lounge sofa.

The party is on Saturday and that gives me a couple of days to prepare. Des is very happy and excited. I've also invited Matthew and his new wife.

We'll announce our engagement to everyone at the party. I know my mother will be very surprised and happy. She likes Andy and his effect on me. After all since the divorce, Andy is the first person I have been able to relate to on so many levels. And the only person I have dated seriously.

I wonder how Andy's family took the news. I think they are happy for him. I wonder if they informed his dad and if so how he reacted. I don't know him. Somehow whenever he was home, Andy never suggested me going over except the one time when they introduced me as Crystal's friend. He seemed okay with that. But how is he going to react now? I don't think he'll be too happy. I'm older than Andy and I have a child by my first marriage. I think Andy's dad is much more of a traditionalist than the rest of his family.

I called my mother and she is happy and is looking forward to seeing Desmond again and also Andy. She likes Andy and she thinks he is good for me. She said we'll talk when she comes. Should I be worried? Life is very strange. When you no longer look for something that is when something fantastic happens. I never thought to fall in love again, but this time it is even better.

AFTER DESMOND'S BIRTHDAY PARTY

SYLVIA

Oh what an evening! My goodness, I never thought I could ever be so happy. All those who are important to me were together. It's been such a long time since I had a party at my place.

Our announcement came as a shock to my family but they were all very glad. My mother couldn't stop beaming all evening long. Gorgeous Meredith – an irrepressible child told me that she was going to be my flower girl because as she put it – there were no other young girls and Des' would not like being a flower boy. She is such a joyous child that looking at her or even thinking about her, makes me smile.

I was a bit worried at first that she might resent me because she is so deeply attached to Andy but as she put it – now she'll have two older sisters instead of only one older sister.

Andy's mum was very nice but a little reserved – as always. She congratulated me and said she thought I'd be good for Andy, if what she's been seeing is anything to go by. I like Andy's mum. She seems to be a very fair and kind person. I think Crystal gets her strength of character from her mother.

I'm rapt with happiness. I'll be Andy's wife and we will love each other forever and forever. Oh I'm so lucky that we met – by a fluke as I only went to that party because Jenny begged me to. She didn't want to go alone. That was my lucky night. It all seems to have happened a long, long time ago. So much has transpired and so much has changed.

Oh it's wonderful to be alive. I'm meeting Andy around 10am. Maybe we'll go to the zoo with Des. He's been asking me to go for a long time. Perhaps Mum and Jack would like to come along.

I'll pack a picnic lunch – just in case. Oh I'm so excited. The world is such a wonderful place. I love Andy more than I ever thought I could love another person. Loving Des is different. He's my son. The love I have for him is different to my feelings for others.

Andy is very lucky that he has siblings he gets along with as I am with mine even though Jack is my half-brother. His father divorced my mother three years ago and then he went back to Brazil to be with his first family. So both Jack and I are so-to-speak – fatherless but my mum fills that void beautifully.

It's funny, but since falling in love with Andy I notice and enjoy simple things like the sky at sunset, the young shoots, the smell of the flowers, the flitting butterflies and the call of the cicadas of an evening. Andy and I have spent many an evening on the balcony sitting and just enjoying the world around us. It's good we share many common interests. Sometimes we walk in the woods or go to the seaside. We usually take Des with us but sometimes we leave him with Andy's family – always when Andy's dad isn't there. Meredith and Des get along like a house on fire. Often she comes over with Andy and the two kids spend time like siblings. Meredith leads and Des follows. I think it's good for both of them to have each other like siblings.

Oh there is the phone ringing. Must be Andy.

CRYSTAL

The engagement dinner went very well. But Dad still doesn't know. We've all decided it's better to break the news to him when he returns home. I have no idea how he'll react but I don't expect that he'll be too pleased.

Well, it's nice that Sylvia's family could also come. Meredith informed all of us that she was going to be the flower girl as Sylvia has no little girl. She also informed us that she wanted real flower petals including red and white rose petals. You just can't be angry with her. She knows her mind and speaks it. She thinks the wedding is tomorrow. When we told her it was not for a while, and that we also needed to speak with Dad about it, she was crestfallen. But why she queried. She couldn't wait!

I'm worried. Andy wants to rush into this marriage. I think they should wait at for a year at least. I don't know the best way to tell Dad. He is going to throw a temper tantrum. I don't know. I'm worried. Andy is too happy. He believes that Dad will be happy for him. I'm not so sure.

Dad likes control and all this happened without his knowledge or permission. Moreover, we had introduced Sylvia as my friend – though that is not really an issue. What I think will be an issue is that she is older than Andy and a divorcee with a young child. Dad is rather harsh and strict about some things. As we always said he belongs to prehistoric times. But maybe everything will be fine and all will go smoothly. I know Mum too is worried. Andy says he'll talk to Dad because it is about time he accepted other people's point of view and their life choices. Andy is not a baby and has the right to choose for himself. Dad has to learn to accept that. I don't know how things are going to work out. I don't know… I'm worried.

THE CONFRONTATION

'Tis all a Chequer-board of Nights and
Days
Where Destiny with Men for Pieces
plays:
Hither and thither moves, mates
and slays
And one by one in the Closet lays.

Edward FitzGerald-
Rubaiyat of Omar Khayyam XLIX

MEREDITH

Oh I hate dad. He beat Andy and made him cry. I wanted to shout at him but Crystal put her hand over my mouth and I couldn't say anything. Then she whispered in my ear that if I loved Andy, I'd go to my room and wait while she spoke to Dad. I nodded and went to my room. Crystal always helps Andy. She'll make Dad stop shouting and hitting Andy. Dad is mean. Why does he always have to hurt Andy? I love Andy much more than Dad. It's good when he goes away. Then Andy doesn't cry or be sad. I love Andy. Tonight I'll let him sleep with my doll Woolly or my koala, Jackson. Jackson came from a place called Australia. I want to go to Australia and be friends with a koala like Jackson.

I whispered to Crystal to please stop Dad from making everything bad again.

CRYSTAL

I repeatedly told Dad to stop it but it only got worse. He said many things that should never have been said. I hate his lack of self- control. He is a bully and its's very hard for Andy to stand up to him.

Andy is gentle and a dreamer. He has never been able to get along with Dad and we all blame Dad for that though I've never said that out loud. Dad lost his temper because Andy refused to do what Dad ordered. He wanted Andy to break up with Sylvia and never see her again. Andy refused. Then he said some very nasty things about Sylvia that made Andy very, very angry. I have never seen Andy lose his temper like this. To make matters even worse Dad took off his slippers and hit Andy with it. We begged him to stop but he didn't until his hand started hurting. Then he ordered Andy to leave the house only in the clothes he was wearing and never come back again. He could go to his room to take his ID card and such things. He was not allowed to take any money with him.

Andy went to his room and locked the door.

I didn't follow him thinking I'd give him some time to get control of himself but I passed in front of his door and said I'd be there in a few minutes.

I went to speak with my mother. She too was appalled. This was totally beyond all our comprehension. How did it degenerate to this stage? It all began when Andy said that he met a girl and fell in love and wanted to marry her. Dad asked him who and Andy told him. From there Dad lost it. For a second I thought he'd have a heart attack. I don't know why he reacted like that.

Mum decided to go and see Andy but his room was locked and he would not answer. So I suggested we use the spare key. I had a bad feeling in my gut.

We opened the door and found Andy asleep on the bed. Something didn't look right. As we looked around the room we found medicine bottles and his sleeping tablet bottle totally empty. We assumed he had taken the pills. So we gave him a lot of water to try and wash out his system and called for the ambulance.

We took him to the hospital where they pumped his stomach. They told us he'd be fine and to pick him up the next morning. Mum and I returned home. Neither of us slept. We prayed for him. Around three in the morning I dozed off but was startled awake with the phone ringing (4 am – I'll never forget that time). I picked up the extension and heard the hospital saying that Andy had had a heart-attack and passed away.

I put down the phone. I couldn't cry. Mum couldn't cry Meredith didn't understand what was happening. She looked bewildered. I have no memory of what Dad said or did that day and the following days. We were all in a daze.

We could not function. It was all beyond our understanding. Andy was supposed to come home in good health. How did this happen?? Why did he die? What went wrong? So many questions and no answers. Mum looked too shocked. I still don't know how she coped. Meredith looked lost and bewildered. She didn't understand what had happened and kept asking when Andy would wake up. I functioned as best as I could to take the burden off Mum. I have no recollection about my father's reaction. Nor do I care to know. He was solely guilty for what happened. Had he considered someone else and not behaved in that grotesque fashion, things might have been very different. We all blame Dad but no one has articulated it. There's not much point in finger pointing now. The fact remains: Andy is dead and soon to go into his final resting place. The world has turned topsy-turvy. We are left to mourn the passing of a bright life. I know I will never, ever forgive Dad for this.

On the third day of his death, they told me later, I had a nervous breakdown.

WAKE UP DEAD

Lo ! Some we loved, the loveliest and the best
That Time and Fate of all their Vintage prest
Have drunk their Cup a Round or two Before
And one by one crept silently to Rest.

Edward FitzGerald-
Rubaiyat of Omar Khayyam XXI

ANDY

My name is Andy Anderson. I went to sleep alive and woke up dead. How could that be? I cannot be dead. This is just a nightmare and soon I'll wake up. But why am I having this nightmare? Ah Yes I remember I was having a confrontation with my dad and I took some sleeping pills to just sleep for a while. Tomorrow morning I will wake up and go to Sylvia's flat and we'll get married and live happily ever after. Ever after – why does that word trouble me? Why is everything so grey and colourless and alien here? I recognise nothing and remember only bits and pieces of who I am and all that.

My body feels weightless but I feel discomfort in my essence like wearing new clothes or being in an unfamiliar place where you keep bumping into things because you don't know the setting. I'm disoriented. I wonder how much time has passed. It's impossible to guess because I don't see any clocks and time seems to have no meaning here.

As I talk I seem to be floating away. I have no control over my limbs that too are too uncoordinated. Everything appears grey and hazy.

Where am I? Perhaps I can wake myself up?

I tried to wake up and now I seem to be losing the threads of my thoughts. Could I really be dead???? Why can't I wake myself up?? Why can't I remember? Why are my memories fading away by the second? There is a feeling of timelessness here? What place is this?? So many questions and no answers!!!

THE AFTERMATH

*Oh Thou, who Man of baser Earth didst
Make,
And who with Eden didst devise the
Snake:
For all the Sin wherewith the Face of
Man
Is blacken'd, Man's Forgiveness give – and take!*

Edward FitzGerald-
Rubaiyat of Omar Khayyam

CRYSTAL

Poor darling mum! Her hair has turned pure white overnight. I don't believe what I know has happened because it's too shocking. We have informed Sylvia and she attended the funeral service. Her pain was palpable. None of us have any words of comfort. We can only say: *Comfort thyself. What comfort is there in me?? (Morte'd' Arthur* – Tennyson). I have no words. Poor mum. Her only son and favourite child!! It is a nasty trick that fate has played on us.

I haven't seen Dad except at the funeral. I can't bring myself to talk to him yet. I blame him. We all do. He should not have done what he did. Andy is not a small child to punish physically or otherwise. And too much was said that should never have been said.

MRS ANDERSON

Crystal has had a serious nervous breakdown. She doesn't eat or drink but has to be force fed or go on the drip. She has not talked at all from the third day of Andy's death. She does not walk or talk but stares up at the ceiling when she is awake. My voice is the only one she occasionally responds too. The doctors all say it will pass. She will be okay. I rarely leave her side. Meredith is like a waif. She sits by Crystal and tells her what is happening but she does not talk or laugh as she used to.

I'm worried about Crystal in spite of the doctors' assurances. It's been three months since her collapse. How much longer is she going to be in this comatose state? What does she think about? We have to have patience and faith that this cup of sadness will also pass as all things in life pass. True, life will never be the same again but we must put our faith in God and survive this terrible time. I must hold on to the hope that soon Crystal will get better and start living.

Some good news at last! Meredith got Crystal to respond verbally. She has slowly started to recover but she still cannot walk or feed herself properly.

THE EPILOGUE

*And when Thyself with shining Foot has
Pass
Among the Guests Star-Scatter'd on the
Grass
And in thy joyous Errand reach the
spot
Where I made one – turn down an empty
Glass!*

TAMAM SHUD – The End

Edward FitzGerald-
Rubaiyat of Omar Khayyam *LXXV*

MRS ANDERSON

Crystal has left home and gone to work overseas. She calls me once or twice a week. I've started worrying a lot about her. She changed drastically after the tragedy. The good thing is that she is strong and has a lot of faith.

Meredith has begun school and is a rather subdued child. She's lost her *joie d' vivre.* We have come a long way in a very short time. Sylvia has gone to live with her mother and brother. She has taken all this very badly. She occasionally calls us.

George is much as he used to be. He travels a lot and when he is home he still drinks a lot. I don't interfere with anything he does.

I read my Bible and find solace in it. The family is fractured. I pass the days as well as I can. I'm tired.

LOSS

AT THE BEGINNING

Perhaps in this neglected spot is laid
Some heart once pregnant with celestial fire
Hands that the rod of empire might have sway'd
Or waked to ecstasy the living lyre.

Elegy written in a Country Churchyard -
Thomas Gray

ANNABELLE AND ALEXANDER

This true life story begins as most true life stories do with a young couple. Alexander and Annabelle were school friends and once they finished their GCE and then 'A' levels they both decided to study literature. Alex wanted to become a professor of literature and Annabelle or Bella as everyone called her, wanted to become a writer. They were both very intelligent people and learning was a hoot for them. Both did extremely well on their GCE exams and their 'A' levels. They were both accepted in their first choice of a university. Alex and Bella were close neighbours. They had grown up together and were quite inseparable. Their families were also close friends.

The kids shared a lot in common especially their love of the environment and all living creatures and their love of poetry. Life was great and loads of fun. Both were only children so they treated each other as siblings do including friendly rivalry and little spats. As time passed and they grew up things started to change. Alex became rather possessive of Bella and did not like other boys showing too much interest in her. Bella loved Alex but not quite in that way. He was her dearest friend and her darling brother. Alex felt differently and that led to trouble. Because neither was violent, their depression took different forms. But more of that later as it happened much later.

At the university both were in the same class and so were together again for most of the day. They got on like a house on fire but there was a slight change – too slight to even notice at first. Bella was a very pretty and vivacious girl and automatically attracted attention. And she was an excellent student. She was very outgoing and bubbly. Alex on the other hand was much more reserved though he too was very good-looking. People often commented around this time that they made a very handsome couple. Bella laughed it off. Not so Alex. He started looking at Bella in a different light. He loved her quirky sense of humour and her ability to always see the positive even in very negative situations. Bella just loved Alex – even when he irritated her by being too possessive. Life was fun and life was good.

Time passed and then one day in April all changed. Alex proposed and Bella said no to the proposal. She loved him truly but not quite in that way. Alex was shattered. All his life Bella had been the centre of his universe. He had thought all along that she felt the same way in spite of the times she dated others. He had closed his eyes and mind and heart to all those indicators.

They continued as before his declaration but something, something intangible had changed between them. Alex became even more possessive. He hated Bella to be away from him. It was a very difficult time for Bella. She loved Alex but did not like his possessiveness. She was a very independent young lady.

To shock her into marrying him, Alex proposed to one of Bella's close friends – Amy. Amy was over the moon and accepted with alacrity. She had long tried to waken his interest. Bella was happy for Alex. Alex was not happy. Soon he started to indulge in recreational drugs – a thing he had never done before. Bella suspected something was off by his strange behaviour at times. But all that would unfold later.

Unknown to Bella, Alex was using heroin and cannabis. His new girlfriend Amy, joined him in this and never tried to stop him. But she used only a little and only sometimes. Alex then started using it regularly but Bella did not know. He made sure to keep this from her. It was their first secret from each other in all the years that they had been friends. Bella did not have any steady boyfriend. She felt it was not the right time for her. Alex's friendship was enough for her.

Alex and Bella continued as usual – studying together spending the evening together, going to the cinema together, going to discoes and social events together etc. Amy knew but did not show any anger or irritation. So Alex assumed it was okay with her. It was not. From being Bella's friend she had turned to disliking Bella. Bella, who meanwhile, was unaware of this continued to regard her as a friend. She just assumed that both Alex and Amy were okay with all the arrangements. If she felt that it was rather unusual, she never said a word about it to anyone.

Then Alex started missing classes. And often when he attended his focus was not like it used to be. He often looked tired and lack-lustre. Bella asked him what the matter was. He told her that he wasn't sleeping well and wasn't eating well either. She asked if he had been to the GP. Alex said he did not need to see the GP. It was just a momentary thing. Bella continued to be worried but didn't push it. She decided to call his mother when she got home.

When Bella called Alex's mother and asked her what was going on and why Alex looked so unwell, his mother told Bella she didn't know and had planned to call Bella and ask her. She also said that Alex was brooding a lot too. Bella promised to find out what she could.

One day, soon after this talk, Alex asked Bella if she wanted to try some recreational drugs - just the two of them together. Bella did not want to say an outright no so she hedged by saying *perhaps at the weekend.* This was so that she could do some research on it. Thanks to technology! They set a date for Saturday evening. They would spend all the time together – like old times. Alex was very happy. His Bella would be with only him for a long time and maybe he would change her mind. Bella was very worried. This was a totally new and unexpected development. She wondered how this had happened. Who had got him into it? How long had it been going on for? Or was it the first time he was going to try it and so he asked her to share the experience with him. Until now he had been as against it as Bella when other friends tried it and had offered them to join in the experiments or regular usage. Bella knew many of the students were users and though it was unlawful, getting drugs was not difficult. The truth is both Bella and Alex had seen what drugs could do in the long run – as exhibited by some of their peers and they hadn't been ready to go down that path. At that time in the early to mid 1970's –it was not such a big thing doing drugs. A lot of people did it and most students had at least tried it at some point.

Bella and Alex had seen how from just trying it occasionally, it became a habit and how it had destroyed the lives of so many. They had agreed a long time ago that they would never go down this path. So Bella was shocked at Alex's suggestion that they try it.

Alex did not invite Amy. He wanted Bella alone to himself. He had only proposed to Amy to make Bella jealous but that had failed. Instead it had backfired. He decided not to get engaged as yet.

BELLA'S RESEARCH

Bella decided to research recreational drugs. This is what she found out about them: Cannabis and Heroin were the most popular and easily available and the cheapest. In the UK it was Cannabis while in the US it was Heroin. A lot of celebrities made drugs very popular by using them. It was an issue between the older and younger generations – most clearly demonstrated by the release of the Beatles – an extremely popular Liverpool band – album in June 1967 – *Sgt Peppers Lonely Hearts Club Band* – an album deeply steeped in drug mysticism.

In the early 1960's Cannabis was very popular and in the 1970's it was replaced by Heroin

This was accompanied by poppers (Amyl nitrate) in the 1960's which became a soft recreational drug in the 1970's as other harder drugs came into use.

All recreational drugs belong to three groups:

- Depressants which induce a sense of relaxation and calm
- Stimulants which induce a feeling of energy and alertness – many users write, paint or produce great works in such a state
- Hallucinogens which induce distortions like hallucinations.

All are habit forming.

Some of the drugs in common use were:

Amphetamines like Speed, Purple Hearts, DEXYS, French Blues and Black Bombers. These drugs began in London's West End and soon became nationwide favourites.

All these drugs were somewhat same in the sense that they altered perception and slowed down the body's responses. Some users became very happy, some became very depressed and some became violent. You didn't know how it would affect you before taking it. But all of these drugs made the users lose their inhibitions. Another effect of drug taking, Bella found out was that you didn't sleep after taking it and you lost your hunger. In due course you lost a lot of weight, your hands started to tremble and you lost concentration. You became more apathetic.

Life was frenetic – at the best, especially for the youth of the newly rich working class. Amphetamines helped them to cram a lot of experience in a weekend – their only free time.

Another drug widely in use was Marijuana which is a highly addictive drug. Still another drug, even worse than Heroin, was Fentanyl which affects the respiratory system. This is much, much stronger than Morphine. It really became most popular in the mid 1970's. This can be smoked, snorted or injected.

LSD (Lysergic Acid Diethyamide-25) or Acid as it was commonly known as was the signature drug for the time. This is an extremely potent conscious expanding drug and it was widely popular in the mid 1970's.

Though drugs were banned they continued to be widely used and easily available as was apparent by the number of young drug users, not just in the UK but also in other Western countries. Since the 1960's when it was at its peak, drug use has not ever stopped. Even today in 2019 drug use is quite widespread.

Bella was shocked. It could not be happening. This must be a nightmare and/or a terrible joke. Soon she'd hear that it was all a trick. Perhaps this must be why Alex was so not himself. He must be taking it more than a one off. She decided to accept his invitation and accost him. She knew he would not tell her a deliberate lie.

She went over to Alex's house and they arranged to do drugs at the weekend so that they'd be fine by Monday and ready for classes. It was right at the end of their university life and getting their degrees.

At his house, first of all Bella tried to talk him out of taking the drug but when she failed, she tried a little with him. Not liking the taste as she was not a smoker, she stopped but stayed while Alex finished his. Bella encouraged Alex to start coming to classes regularly. He promised to be there on Monday. Bella was happy. She promised to pass by for a short while the next day.

On the next Saturday morning she went over to visit Alex and they spent the day together. On Sunday Alex came over to Bella's house and they listened to music, danced and talked shop.

Bella's mum had prepared Alex's favourite dishes so they had dinner together with Bella's family and then Alex went home. Both Bella and Alex were happy. Bella because she thought that now Alex would stop the drugs and Alex because he thought Bella would accept his proposal.

The next few months were fine. They did not discuss their relationship which was now seemingly as it was before the proposal. It was the calm before the storm. Alex reduced his drug taking drastically as he was mostly with Bella. Amy said not a word but her anger was all directed at Bella though Bella had told her Alex was like a brother to her. Amy was very jealous even though they often invited her to join them either at Alex's house or Bella's house or when they went dancing or to the cinema. Amy came but did not participate in the conversation much. Her resentment grew.

One warm August day, Alex again proposed and Bella said she loved him dearly but could not marry him. No, there wasn't anyone else. And again it began. Alex started missing classes and went back on drugs. Bella didn't know what to do, so she asked her mother if she should accept Alex's proposal to make him happy. Her mother said that that sort of a relationship never worked out in the long run. It would be better if they stopped seeing each other so often. This was because Bella used to visit Alex or Alex visited her everyday. He seemed to have forgotten Amy. Sometimes Amy came to visit Bella when she knew Alex was there. It was a bit uncomfortable for Bella because Alex paid no attention to Amy.

Exam time got nearer. Their visits to each other lessened especially as Alex had withdrawn from the degree. Bella concentrated on her studies.

Exam time came and went. Bella did extremely well but before the results were out something happened, something that was to change not just Bella's life but her perceptions. She got a frantic call from Alex's mum to come over immediately. Alex had collapsed and they had called the ambulance. Bella went over. She hadn't seen Alex only for about 10 days. He looked very pale and frail. Why? She asked his mother. She said he was doing a lot of drugs and eating less and less. Bella decided that when he came back she'd try to get him off drugs again. Alex was in hospital for about a week. He came home looking much like his old self. Everyone was very pleased. They had a lovely meal and sat together watching a film.

Next morning when Bella went over to see Alex he looked hung over and asked Bella not to visit him anymore. He said she made him unhappy, even to look at her. Bella asked him why and he said it was because she was not in love with him and wouldn't marry him. Bella left.

Bella kept in touch with his mum but she told Bella that he was getting sicker and sicker. Bella went to see him. He looked like a wraith. His mother told Bella that he couldn't eat. The amphetamine, Acid and LSD had destroyed his stomach lining and badly burned his oesophagus. He was on a drip. His oesophagus could not be repaired. Bella cried. It was all so sad. Bella took to visiting him every day and stayed reading to him, listening to music or just holding his hand every day. She only went home for the basic necessities. Alex looked happy as long as she was with him, holding his hand, listening to his favourite music or just talking to him.

On 24 December 1977 Alex's mother called to tell Bella that Alex was in hospital again. Bella left for the hospital. Her parents couldn't go with her as they had guests expected any minute.

Alex died on 25 December 1977 at 6:30am. What a waste of a wonderful intellect and a gorgeous person. And while the world celebrated Christmas cheer, Alex's family and Bella mourned the tragedy of a bright spirit extinguished before his time.

Bella never forgot Alex. Through all the years without his presence, she remembered him and hated drugs with a passion. Later in life she decided to research drugs. She understood Alex better as a result. She became a strong advocate against drug usage. She wrote about it and gave talks especially to young adults who are more prone to using it, usually due to peer pressure.

BELLA'S SECOND RESEARCH

Bella could not and did not forget Alex. As the years passed she became a strong advocate against drug use. She didn't want another family to suffer what Alex's did. Alex was always like a brother and best friend rolled in one, even though he had not thought so towards the end. It was her duty in Alex's memory to do what she could to help others in similar circumstances.

AUSTRALIA

There are free drug injecting rooms in Sydney and Melbourne but users must be

- ❖ Over 18 years of age,
- ❖ Already dependant on drugs,
- ❖ Must not be accompanied by children
- ❖ Must not be intoxicated when they come in
- ❖ Under supervision
- ❖ Must give their personal information including overdose history and medical treatment history (care in case of overdosing is available in the after-care rooms)
- ❖ Users are not allowed to go back to the injecting rooms following immediately after an over-dosing incident
- ❖ Must not traffic in drugs on the premises
  However recently in Melbourne a worker at the injecting premises was caught trafficking in drugs and is currently under investigation (2019)
- ❖ The centre also helps with housing, social welfare and legal issues

Safe injecting rooms are also available in a number of Western countries:

SWITZERLAND

In 1986 Berne opened the very first premises for safe drug use in order to get users off the streets. They provided cafeterias for drug users with showers, change of clothes, health provisions and health and social welfare. Some rules that users are expected to follow strictly on these premises are:

❖ Alcohol cannot be sold on these premises
❖ Drug-dealing is strictly forbidden
❖ The user must be 18 years or over
❖ Must be a dependant drug user with official documentation to that effect
❖ Casual users are not allowed on the premises

On the premises there are separate places for injecting, snorting/sniffing and smoking drugs.

CANADA

Vancouver has the only legal drug consumption premises in the whole of North America. It functions under a special exemption from Canadian drug laws. The health minister had rejected extending the exemption but the Canadian Supreme Court ruled in favour of the premises staying open.

The users here all remain anonymous and unlike most drug use rooms, there are no set criteria for entering and using the facility. However the rooms are also used for research into drug use. It is not mandatory and users can choose not to participate.

There are 12 booths for users equipped with syringes, cookers and tourniquets and chill-out lounges for those who wish to detox or begin the process of detoxification before they move into rehabilitation.

THE NETHERLANDS

Church-operated social care premises were open in 1990 but it was only in 1996 consumption rooms came to be established by law.

By 2010 there were 37 consumption rooms in 25 different cities in the Netherlands. These premises also catered to a broad range of social and medical care to the users.

- ❖ The users were asked to sign a contract detailing the rules to be adhered to on the premises
- ❖ They were asked to have their own drugs on them
- ❖ Time spent in the room by the user was limited

There are separate rooms for injecting and smoking.

GERMANY

There were already drug taking rooms in Frankfurt and Hamburg because of the large number of users well before 2000 when they were formally legalised. There are 26 rooms in 17 cities of Germany. The users must adhere to the rules in each user room at all times. The premises offers the following:

- ❖ Clean drug use implements are offered
- ❖ On-site counselling is available for those who want it
- ❖ Affordable meals are on offer
- ❖ Free condoms
- ❖ Free shower rooms
- ❖ Free laundry service
- ❖ People under opioid-replacement therapy are not allowed to use these rooms
- ❖ New injectors are not allowed
- ❖ Intoxicated people are not allowed use of these rooms

Besides these countries drug injecting rooms are also available in **Spain, Luxembourg** and **Norway**. They differ in the extent of services offered. This policy of making such premises available to drug users aims at reducing the health-associated risks and offers an on-the-spot treatment to emergency situations. It also aims at taking drug users off the streets – at least while using it.

Drugs are bad. Fullstop. One should avoid ever taking it. It is very easy to get addicted and very difficult to break that addiction. It affects you mentally, physically psychologically and emotionally. For a short-term-euphoria you pay a very high price. In our modern world we have advanced to being able to treat addiction to a limit. Drug addiction is still a very big and bad problem in all Western societies. No disappointment, however bad means that we should turn to drugs. They are the bane of modern society. Many bright young girls and boys destroy a fruitful and successful life if and when they go down this path. They break the hearts of those that love them – pain that never really goes away. And when it is an only child, just think how empty the parents' lives become.

Alex's mother died of stroke two years later. His father survived his mother by seven months. Bella became a very successful teacher in Alex's memory. She went on to fall in love with a wonderful man and marry him and they have a very happy family life. No one in that family does or did drugs. – except Bella that one time long, long ago. She named her first son Alex.

NAOMI

She walks in beauty, like the night
Of cloudless climes and starry skies;
And all that's best of dark and bright
Meet in her aspect and her eyes
Thus mellow'd to that tender light
Which heaven to gaudy day denies.

She walks in Beauty – Lord Gordon Byron

PROLOGUE

My name is Alice. Strange things always happen to me. Wonderful, wondrous things also happen to me. I think I attract the unusual. I am an only child and so lonely from the start though I never realised that then. I have always loved books and that has not changed now that I am old and grey. One of the highlights of my life was meeting and getting to know and to love Naomi. She was the first real friend and the only mentor I have ever had. Naomi was one of the nicest, loveliest people it has been my privilege to know. She did not really belong to this world of sin and corruption. The world, I think fears the pure soul and so tries to destroy it and sometimes succeeds.

I was a good friend to Naomi as Naomi was to me. We met in a curious way under curious circumstances. I was a rather shy and awkward teenager. My books were much more important to me than friends. Books were my friends. School was okay. I liked knowledge and liked to learn. I especially liked Biology. Living creatures fascinated me. I could sit by a rock pool and watch by the hour. But I digress. One day I was at the library, which by the way was one of my favourite places, getting some books. I read something – now I forget what, and I laughed out loud breaking the silent concentrated atmosphere of that hallowed place. Someone grabbed my arm and hauled me out of the library and she said *now laugh but first share your delight with me. I need to laugh too.* I was stunned. Such a thing had never happened to me. Before me was a beautiful young woman small boned and slight, just a little taller than me. I think my mouth fell open because she started to laugh. Her laughter was so infectious that I had to join in. Once the paroxysm of laughter passed, she introduced herself as Naomi. She said she had seen one of the librarians bearing down on me and so she dragged me out. I thanked her and told her my name. I liked her immediately and immensely. I'm like that - I take instantaneous likes and dislikes.

Naomi's laughter was like the tinkling of little bells. When she laughed, she laughed whole-heartedly and you could not but join in. It was that infectious! You didn't need to know why she was laughing in order to join in. I think she was the happiest person I have ever known in spite of how sad her life really was. She knew how to extract the joy and ignore the sorrow that we are born to experience. For me she was the perfect medicine. She changed me in an intrinsic way. I became more like her because she was the only real friend I had or have ever had. We spent a lot of time at her flat because she had duties to perform. The times when we were apart were school times, and dinner times. I usually did my homework at her place while she prepared dinner for her family.

PART I

Who was Naomi?

Naomi was Naomi – a beautiful, pure, gentle unusual soul in a contaminated world.

Naomi had a brother and sister. Her brother lived in Spain. They talked on the phone from time to time. He was much older than her and – and well, boring! Her sister lived in Glasgow with her family. She met them from time to time when Naomi went to visit. Naomi was the youngest of them all. She was only 22 when I met her. I was 15 and getting ready for my GCE. Now I am old and Naomi has been murdered and dead for a long, long time. But again I digress.

Naomi married when she was 17 years old. It had something to do with property and her brother-in-law's greed. She never really talked about it and I never asked because that would have been a very intrusive question. She had 2 sons. They were gorgeous. One was a year old and the other was three years old. The older was called Thomas and the younger was called Alfred. They were very good kids. I loved playing with them. Her husband was John. He was okay. They lived walking distance from our house and so I was there more often than at home. Since meeting Naomi, home had become a lonely place. My mum was busy with her societies and my father with his work. Before I met Naomi, I was quite lonely. After I met her and she befriended me, all that changed. Naomi became my friend, sister and mentor rolled in one person. She taught me not to be so judgemental and serious. She taught me values and she shared many of my passions like reading books that taught me something, and enjoying and caring for the natural world and its inhabitants, valuing all life - nature, birds and animals and to laugh at, from the simplest to the most complex of things. We laughed at a ladybird that kept falling over until we picked her up and put her onto the leaf. We laughed at the dog fighting with a ball. We looked in awe and admired the sunset, a flower slowly opening to the world which it would inhabit for a short time before decay and death took that beautiful flower. We admired the glistening diamond-like perfection of the early morning dew on leaves and other such things. We talked about everything – frivolous to very serious things, about life, love death, friendship, sacrifice etc. etc. I loved her with all my heart. I loved her boys too. They were very cute and often very funny. I behaved like a comedian around them. It made them laugh. I think those were some of the happiest times of my life. Everything was so innocent and untouched by pain or sin or decay or murder.

PART II

THE INTERIM

In summer we would go on picnics with the children. Those were lovely times too. The boys loved the freedom of running in the meadow. Once a hare jumped right over the picnic basket and we split our sides with laughter. The hare executed a perfect jump.

I often took my books to do my homework at her place and when I finished, we sat around and talked about anything and everything. Often, we used to read the same book and then discuss it with each other. That was a lot of fun.

Life was fun and good and interesting. I think that was the happiest time of my life before other things intervened.

Soon I began university. I decided to study microbiology. The subject interested me. I wanted to do something tangible for society and I thought this would be a good way to do so. Naomi said she was impressed and encouraged me all the way.

For Naomi's 25th birthday I threw her a surprise party and then we had our own celebration – just our two families the next evening. We went out to a wonderful dinner. It was great.

Then Naomi went overseas as her husband got a posting in Spain. We wrote to each other everyday and called each other on alternate days. It was still very good. We were in constant touch and could share all what happened. Distance did not matter. Naomi loved Spain. She used to share with me all the places she visited and many of the people she met. But she missed home a lot too. Her boys too, missed home and all their friends even though they made some new friends there. They went to the International school in Spain, so language was not a barrier.

Even though Naomi and I were in close touch, I still missed her. I missed our spending time together, sharing the funny, quirky, serious things together. You can't really share the little things always on the phone. But such is life. You've got to take the bad with the good. And the best thing is nothing lasts forever. Naomi said that it was a one- off posting for her husband and they would be back latest by the next year. He had been posted to close some specific deals. The year would pass fast. Already four months had gone by.

Naomi sent me some gifts every now and then. They were all beautiful. One was a Spanish brooch studded with semi-precious stones. I loved that brooch and used it as much as I could. The brooch reminded me of her - delicate, beautiful and enduring.

Then the wonderful call came. Naomi and her family were returning. She gave me her flight number, date, time etc. I had her flat cleaned and a meal prepared for them. Then I went to the airport to get them. It was a wonderful reunion. We were both euphoric. Life was going to go back to normal. We had so much to talk about. But I thought it would be only fair to give them a couple of days to recover.

I was very excited. I wanted to hear all her news and really how it had been in a foreign country. What did they eat? Who did the cooking? Did they have help? Did she learn any Spanish? I had a thousand questions for her. But that could all wait.

The days passed slowly and tediously. But they needed the time to get over their jet lag. I went to my classes and had to concentrate which was a good thing. We had some exams coming up and I wanted to keep up my grades. Moreover, I enjoyed University life. I was learning a lot and I was even more convinced that I wanted to become a Microbiologist and do something good for humanity. But I won't bore you with all that. This is specifically about one topic – Naomi. Don't get me wrong. We both had other friends but they were not as important or close to us as we were to each other. We both felt that there must have been a very strong connection between us in a previous lifetime. Perhaps we had been sisters.

Then Naomi called and asked me to go over. I went and we talked and laughed for a long time. She told me some funny experiences she had while trying to speak in Spanish. She said that everyone had started to laugh. And when they translated what she had in fact said, she too started to laugh. It was funny.

It was really nice to have Naomi back. Life went back to being normal and good again.

THE PASSAGE OF TIME

Time passed. Naomi's boys grew up and went to University. I finished my degree and became an assistant microbiologist. I loved my job. The only fly in the ointment was I had less time to spend with Naomi but we still spoke every day and spent most of the weekend and holidays together.

But all good things come to an end. I don't know if the gods get jealous or what. Sometimes the pain is so intense that tears don't come. And the wound doesn't heal.

On a sunny day - the date and day and month are etched in my mind – It was Saturday 21st June we got a call that changed all our lives. Someone had broken into Naomi's flat and shot her twice – once in the head and once in the heart. Nothing was taken.

The police said it was a home invasion. There had been a series of that in recent days.

It was a pointless, senseless, meaningless murder. May the perpetrator rot in hell through all eternity! I lost my best friend and the world lost one of its purest souls.

So passed away one of the purest souls and left us all to mourn.

I shall never forget the free and pure spirit that was Naomi. She was a bright light in a dark, dark world.

A COLD CASE

The police never caught the perpetrator. They said they were investigating all the leads and the cases of home invasion. But they seem to have got nowhere. Meanwhile Naomi is in her cold and lonely grave. And all those she left behind mourn her passing. She was a streak of pure light in an otherwise dark, sombre and cold world. If I close my eyes, I can still see her laughing face – even after so many, many years have passed by,

Naomi is now reduced to a numbered box and is now a cold case. From time to time I inquired about the progress of the case but got nothing from the authorities. So I'll have to wait until they finally catch the perpetrator.

EPITAPH

Full many a gem of the purest ray serene
That dark, unfathom'd caves of ocean bear:
Full many a flower is born to blush unseen,
And waste its sweetness on the desert air.

Elegy written in a Country Churchyard –
Thomas Gray

SHATTERED

When the lamp is shattered
The light in the dust lies dead
When the cloud is scattered
The rainbow's glory is shed

Posthumous Poems
by Percy Bysshe Shelley

PROLOGUE

Georgina Hill was a happy, healthy child and grew to be a happy, healthy young adult. We were in school together and then in university in the same department. Gina was lots of fun, but by the middle of the first year at university, she started missing a lot of lectures. She was often sick and always tired. She started losing weight – fast. I asked her why she was dieting since she wasn't fat to begin with. She replied that she wasn't dieting but somehow, she seemed to be losing weight. Perhaps that was why she was so tired. The doctor prescribed supplements, and a richer diet. But nothing changed. Gina kept being tired, losing weight and feeling a severe, general malaise.

Back to the doctor she went. Then to the hospital for tests! And more tests and still more tests. The year was 1974 when medicine was not as advanced as it is today.

Gina's blood test results proved extremely harrowing. The doctors said she probably had Leukaemia which is a type of cancer that affects the blood system and the bones. Everyone was shattered. It was the very first time any of us came face-to-face with this. We were so shocked that almost by unspoken consensus we all decided to ignore the results. Poor Gina and her family! They could not bury their heads in the sand. They had to face the sharp and bleak reality. The doctors said that they had to do many more tests before they could be absolutely positive.

FRIENDS FOREVER

Jessica and Juliana were twin sisters and Georgina was their friend. The three girls went to Kindergarten together and progressed to primary school together and then secondary school. They often forgot that they were friends. They felt more like siblings. When they finished secondary school Georgina's family moved to another city which was Georgina-home town. Georgina opted to stay behind and study with her friends in the university of their choice. They girls took a flat among the three of them because Gina refused to be separated from the other two girls. Their parents thought it was a good idea. They would take care of each other and learn to be somewhat independent in a safe setting. Life was good and great fun. Juliana and Georgina studied Literature at the university, while Jessica studied political science. The girls were still inseparable though Georgina somehow was a mite friendlier with Jessica than Juliana. No one minded or was resentful. Both Jessica and Georgina sometimes found Juliana too far up in the clouds and with a fragile connection to reality. The other two were more down-to-earth. Time passed and they were happy or sad as the situation warranted. They went to discoes and had crushes though nothing serious. Gina and Jessica both loved Elvis Presley and had a big crush on him. Juliana had her crush on Cliff Richard. All three also had a crush on the Beatles. This was a good kind of crush. It kept them out of harm's way.

At weekends they went to Jessica and Juliana's parents or to stay with Gina's parents. In both places they relaxed and were much cosseted. But when life is perfect and couldn't be better, there is a sharp sting that reminds us that we are human and our very humanity renders us pawns of fate, unable to change the course that was pre-set for us. All our laughter can turn to tears in the blink of an eye and all our hopes dashed, fears magnified, sorrows multiplied. But I digress and skip too far ahead. It is just because reality stands at my elbow, nudging me, and will not let me be free of the unpalatable truth.

All three girls enjoyed university life and they participated in many of the functions and clubs. But none of them wanted to be away from the other two for any period of time. All their other friends knew that if you wanted to be friends with any one of them, you had to take on the trio. They fell whole-heartedly into university life. They enjoyed the studies and the extra-curriculum activities. They mooned over one or another person, as young girls will. It was all a part of growing up and becoming responsible adults.

The first and second year of university passed as in a dream. The girls were content. Then Gina started missing classes. It was nothing serious. She said she was tired and would join them later. Nothing to worry about! But things got worse, not better. Gina started to lose weight and often felt listless. Jessica and Juliana called Gina's parents. They said they'd come down the following week as nothing untoward had happened. Gina probably needed a break and perhaps they'd go overseas for a change of scene. Gina's mother did ask if Gina was in love as girls often feel depressed and lose weight if it is unrequited love but the other two said that wasn't the case. Gina was heart-whole and fancy free. All of them were actually! Gina's parents were relieved. There must be an organic reason for Gina's feeling unwell. Maybe overwork at the university as all three girls were very good students, diligent in their desire to do well.

Gina's parents decided to take her overseas for a holiday. They knew she could catch up and Jessica and Juliana would keep her back.

None of the girls were too excited. It was the first time in aeons that they were going to be separated. Even worse was that Gina was unwell. The only good thing about this trip was the hope that Gina would come back her own happy and healthy self.

Jessica and Juliana could not go due to exams. But the girls promised to stay in close touch.

So Gina went overseas with her parents.

ATHENS, GREECE

Gina's parents took her to Athens as this was a place the two families had come together before and the three girls – Gina, Jessica and Juliana had enjoyed themselves thoroughly. Gina's parents thought that the memories, the sun, the sea and the lovely food would soon make Gina be herself again. And at first that is just what happened. The only fly in the ointment was that she desperately missed Juliana and Jessica. They had always but always been everywhere together from the time they were tiny tots.

Once again they did some of the sight that Gina loved so well. By day they lazed on the beach and at night they had lovely moonlit strolls by the water. Gina often talked about Jessica and Juliana. She bought gifts for them and three bikini-suits – same colour and same design for the three of them. Funnily enough they were the same size and often exchanged clothes. As I said before they were more like sisters than best friends. Gina sent Jessica and Juliana a postcard a day recording all what she had done that day. Even apart, the girls were together. It looked and felt like a storybook world that they inhabited. That is not to say that they never argued or got upset with each other - they did but it was a momentary thing and they soon got over it – whatever 'it' might be.

Gina started eating better and looking better and in no time at all it was time to return. Gina was very impatient to catch up with her friends. Life had righted itself and all was well. Gina's parents felt that they had been right to give Gina a break from her studies. The break from University seemed to have done her a world of good. She was her own bubbly self again. They felt vindicated for their actions every time they looked at their only child. Gina had gained back the weight she had lost and looked fit and healthy. They put it all down to the stresses of university life.

On Saturday they flew back home. Gina was impatient to get back and meet up with her two friends. Gina immediately called Jessica and Juliana and they agreed to meet up in a couple of hours.

Gina: *I have so much to tell you. I really missed you girls. It wasn't quite as much fun as it would have been all together. Never mind - next time.*

Jessica & Juliana together: *Missed you too. Can't wait to tell you our news. You won't believe who's become a couple!!*

Gina*: Bye till then. Ciao*

Jessica & Juliana*: Ciao*

THE NEWS

The next couple of weeks were good. Gina kept up her weight and did not complain of fatigue. But she kept catching one cold after another and started bruising very easily just by bumping into something – not even hard. She also started to have spontaneous bruising and occasional nosebleeds – things she had never had before. It was worrying and sometimes quite embarrassing. Gina never knew when some embarrassing thing might occur and though Jessica and Juliana tried to cover up for her, they were worried about her. The girls insisted and finally the three decided for Gina to see her doctor. That evening they made Gina call her mother and the girls told her about their concerns. Gina's mum said she'd also be there for the doctor's appointment. Maybe Gina needed a longer break and then the Doctor could write a letter to the department and request time off for her due to health concerns.

They got an appointment with the doctor. Gina had her check -up. Everything seemed to be okay so the doctor gave her some multi -vitamins and asked her to have a fasting blood test just to make sure that all was well. Nothing seemed to be seriously wrong but the doctor was a little concerned with her bruising so easily. He thought it could be because of her recent weight loss, before her holiday to Greece. The nosebleeds and flu symptoms could be due to her allergies. Still to be sure, he asked for a fasting blood test.

The next morning Gina, Jessica and Juliana went for Gina's blood test before going to their classes. The girls were in a great mood, exchanging all their news and just hanging out together – as was usual.

When things go too well – something untoward generally happens. The bubble bursts. So it was in this case. Gina got a call from the Doctor with an immediate appointment. The doctor's secretary asked Gina to bring along a support person. All three girls got worried and decided to go together. Under Jessica and Juliana's prompting, Gina called and told her mother about the appointment. Her mother said she'd pass by the flat later that day.

At the doctor's the girls went in together. The doctor looked worried and he kept looking at the blood report. Then he said:

Doctor: *Well, Georgina, I've got your blood report here. I need to do a few more tests before I give my diagnosis. Your white blood cells seem to be rather high. No need to worry at this stage. I need you to go in to the hospital for the next set of tests as soon as possible. I'll give you a referral for the blood specialist there.*

All three girls got very upset at this stage and Gina asked him what was so important or rather bad about the blood results.

The doctor repeated that her white blood cell counts were higher than he liked and he wanted to see why. The next set of results would tell him more and what to do. There was no need to worry at this stage.

Of course this made the girls even more worried. As soon as they returned to the flat they called Gina's mother and told her what the doctor had said.

Next morning the girls all took the day off from their classes. Gina informed her department that she was going into hospital for tests and may have to be there overnight. Gina's mother took them to the hospital. Gina left the overnight bag in the car thinking it would take just a couple of minutes for the test. She handed the referral to the Triage nurse and after they took her temperature, blood pressure and pulse asked her how she felt. Then they admitted her into the hospital. Jessica, Juliana and Gina's mum went in with her.

Gina's mother asked the nurse what the test was for. The nurse simply said not to worry, they just wanted to be sure that all was well with Gina and the high white blood count had a perfectly reasonable explanation. A nurse came and took blood. She informed them the results would be ready within 2 hours. Gina's mother and, Juliana and Jessica all wanted to wait until Gina was released.

Though all of them were each worried, none of them wanted to open the topic so they simply talked inanities while waiting for the result. To lighten the mood, Jessica and Juliana teased Gina that the Doc had a crush on her and other such silly things.

Time dragged on and finally the results and a doctor came. He introduced himself and said he was a specialist in blood diseases. He first asked Gina what was the matter with her and her recent medical history. He also asked her if she knew why her doctor had sent her to the specialist. He asked her a lot of questions. Then he said her white blood cells showed an abnormally high count. He wished to carry out some special new tests before making any prognosis. Gina's mother was very worried and asked what he suspected. He said he would let her know his diagnosis after the new tests. And he left.

A nurse and an orderly came in and took Gina for her tests. The three women sat and said not a word for a few minutes then Juliana said: *What do you think is the matter? Why this hide and seek business? Why couldn't he tell us what he thought?*

Jessica echoed her. Gina's mother said: *Girls, he probably wants to be absolutely sure and does not want to worry us. Perhaps she picked up something when we went to Greece and she'll get a course or two of antibiotics and all will be well again. Maybe there's nothing to get worried about.*

Gina's mum was trying to reassure herself as much as the girls. They waited talking sporadically. Finally after almost an hour Gina returned. Again they waited for the doctor to come and give them his diagnosis.

When he came, he asked everyone to be calm. All our blood pressure shot up. First he asked if there was or had been in cancer in the family. Gina's mum said no. Then he said that Gina had Leukaemia. However the cancer was in its initial stage and could be controlled for some time at least. She could lead a normal life for many years he said.

They kept Gina overnight and next morning, Gina's mother and her two friends came and took her back to the flat, which is where she wanted to go. The girls sat around and comforted each other and talked and talked and talked some more.

LIVING WITH LEUKAEMIA

The girls decided to read up all they could about leukaemia. They would read different bits of information, pool in what they learnt and then it would not be so frightening. The word cancer has very negative connotations and in order to deal with it one has to demystify it. And that's what the girls decided to do.

GEORGINA'S REPORT:

I read that Leukaemia is a kind of Cancer that affects the blood forming cells and tissues and bone marrow cells and tissues of the lymphatic system of the body. I read there are some cancers in this category that affect children only, some both children and adults and some only affect adults.

Leukaemia usually involves the white blood cells. The problem originates in the bone marrow where some blood cells become malignant, do not develop properly and multiply in an uncontrolled way, outstripping the red blood cells. The cells can no longer function properly. These cells are important in fighting infections but when a person has Leukaemia these cells behave in an abnormal way because the bone marrow which produces these cells produces cells that can no longer function normally. The number of white blood cells produced outstrips the red blood cells and results in a lack of blood platelets which are necessary for clotting. People having leukaemia bleed easily and excessively or develop pinprick bleeds. The normal white cells fight pathogens but in the abnormal white cells this function is suppressed or it becomes dysfunctional. So the immune system cannot fight even simple infection.

There are many symptoms that doctors look at when diagnosing Leukaemia. They don't all have to be present but along with blood tests and other tests for cancer may indicate the presence of cancerous cells. Some of the indications are the following symptoms:

Constant fatigue, tiredness and weakness
Unexplained weight loss
Infected tonsil
Mouth sores
Diarrhoea
Life-threatening pneumonia
Unexplained fevers
Frequent infections
Bone pain and/or tenderness
Swollen lymph nodes
Enlarged liver or spleen
Easy bleeding and bruising
Recurrent nose bleeds
Excessive night sweats
Tiny red spots on the skin
Opportunistic infections

A person does not need to show all these symptoms in order to have leukaemia. Some of the symptoms become apparent as the disease progresses.

I also read that there are many other types of leukaemia that can affect people.

Girls you see some of this applies to me. I could not read any further. I know it is good to demystify the disease. Then it appears less frightening. One other thing I read that gives me hope is that it may be treatable though difficult and costly. Because it is a relatively new disease not a lot of work has yet been done on it.

JESSICA'S REPORT:

Scientists don't really know the exact causes of leukaemia but they do know that it attacks the lymphatic system which comprises of the lymph nodes, the spleen, thymus, lymph systems, the tonsils and the adenoid glands. It is believed to be caused because of genetic factors and environmental factors. But not all people with a genetic predilection to cancer get it and many who do get it do not have the genetic problems that are supposed to be a cause of cancer. In other words, they don't really know why someone gets it, I think.

According to doctors the following are the risk factors but as I mentioned before there is no cut and dried rule as to who gets it or why.

Risk factors

➢ Previous chemotherapy and radiation therapy for cancer treatment of any kind may lead to Leukaemia. This, Gina, does not apply to you. You've never had such therapy or treatment.

➢ Genetic disorders like Downs syndrome or other types of genetic abnormalities may be an important factor in causing Leukaemia. Again this does not apply to you

➢ Exposure to certain chemicals like benzene, which is a component of gasoline and used quite widely in the chemical industry. This too, Gina, is not applicable in your case.

➢ Cigarette smoking. This increases the risk of myelogenous leukaemia. But we don't smoke so that does not apply to us.

➢ Previous family history of leukaemia among family members, increases the risk of contracting leukaemia. This does not apply to you either.

However most people with one or many of the above do not contract Leukaemia whereas people without any such risks may and do contract Leukaemia. Gina, you can't have Leukaemia as none of these risk factors applies to you. Maybe they'll find out that it was a wrong diagnoses and all's clear. After all no one in your family has had any form of cancer. We'll hold on to that thought.

Gina, Jessica & Juliana *together: Amen to that.*

JULIANA'S REPORT

I looked at the classification of Leukaemia. Most doctors agree that classification is based on the speed at which the leukaemia progresses or which blood cells it attacks. There are two main classes of Leukaemia:

Myeloid
Lymphocytic
These are subdivided into acute or chronic
Speed of progression

> **Acute Leukaemia** – *in which the abnormal blood cells are immature blood cells called blasts. These do not carry out their normal functions and multiply very rapidly which makes the disease get worse faster. This is an aggressive type of leukaemia and needs quick intervention*
> **Chronic Leukaemia** *There are a number of types of chronic Leukaemia. Some produce an overabundance of cells while others produce too few. This type involves mature blood cells which replicate slowly and can function normally for a time. This type of Leukaemia can go undetected for a long time.*

The other classification of Leukaemia is based on the type of white blood cells that are affected:

> **Lymphocytic Leukaemia.** *This type of leukaemia affects the lymphoid cells or lymphocytes which form the lymphatic tissue in the body. The lymphatic tissue makes up the immune system of our body*
> **Myelogenous Leukaemia.** *This type affects the myeloid cells. These cells produce the red and white blood cells as well as the platelet-producing cells*

The major types of Leukaemia are as follows:

> **Acute lymphocytic leukaemia** *(ALL). This is the commonest kind of leukaemia and usually affects children. However it can also affect adults*
> **Acute myelogenous leukaemia** *(AML). This too is a common kind of leukaemia. It can affect both children and adults. It is also the commonest type of acute leukaemia that affects adults.*
> **Chronic Lymphocytic Leukaemia** *(CLL). This is the commonest type of leukaemia that affects adults and that can remain undetected for years. The person may feel well for years without medication*

- ➤ **Chronic Myelogenous Leukaemia** *(CML). This type of leukaemia mainly affects adults. A person with this kind of leukaemia can have the disease for years and suddenly it flares up fast as the cells multiply very quickly.*
- ➤ **Other types.** *There are other rarer types like the hairy cell leukaemia, myleodyplastic syndromes and myeloprolifertive disorders.*

Jessica*: Look let's put this aside and talk about other things. Gina what would you like to do now?*
Gina: *let's listen to some music. What shall we wear to Sharon's engagement party? It's only 2 weeks away. Perhaps we should go shopping tomorrow*
Jessica and Juliana*: That sounds good. Let's dress the same as usual.*

The next day the girls went shopping and bought identical dresses in pale blue. They tried to push aside the bad news and concentrate on good things that Gina could enjoy. All strenuous things were out. Time passed but always at the back of their minds was Gina's situation.

They went to Sharon's engagement but stayed a short while as Gina felt very tired.

The girls fell into a routine. When Gina was well, she attended classes at the university. At other times Jessica and Juliana brought her up-to-date on everything. On those days the girls finished their lectures and spent the rest of the time together.

Gina suddenly got worse and she needed blood transfusion. She was in hospital overnight. Jessica and Juliana waited as long as they were allowed. Next morning they decided to skip their lectures and visit Gina. She was allowed to go home around noon. Her parents came to take her home. Jessica and Juliana said they'd follow in a couple of hours giving the family some time together. Gina wanted to stay at the flat with the girls. Her parents agreed – whatever Gina wanted was fine for them. The three girls were closer than ever and spent as much time as they could together. Gina's parents came to the flat everyday to be with Gina when the girls were at the university. Gina wanted to be in the flat during this time.

Gina got worse. She lost a lot of weight and was always tired. She stopped her classes. The leukaemia progressed much more rapidly. She started losing weight and started becoming very thin and fragile. By mutual consensus the girls did not talk about it anymore. She needed transfusion more often. Right after her transfusion, she felt better for a week then three days then a couple of days. The Leukaemia started to progress faster and faster. Gina looked like a wraith. She became all skin and bones only, extremely pale and suffered from pain everywhere.

On a Sunday morning Gina passed away. Life changed forever for those who loved her. They kept her memory alive by remembering her. Gina's mother asked the girls to visit her whenever they could so they could talk about Gina. The girls did so. It was a way of recovery for all of them. Every week the girls left a pale pink rose bud on her grave to signify her early death. And every year on Gina's death anniversary the two sisters met up to honour Gina's memory.

Jessica, when she married and had a daughter named her Georgina and Juliana named her daughter Gina. Gina had been much more than a friend. She had been a sister of their hearts and so she will forever be remembered as such. When the sisters got together they always talked about Gina. The passing of time softened the wounds but did not fully heal it. They regularly visited Gina's parents once a week and if they were away then they sent letters and postcards. Gina's mother treated them as her daughters as she used to do when Gina was there.

On Gina's grave the girls asked her parents if they could put this epitaph for Gina.

EPITAPH

Strew on her roses, roses
And never a spray of yew!
In quiet she reposes:
Ah, would that I did too!

Her mirth the world required;
She bathed it in smiles of glee
But her heart was tired, tired,
And now they let her be.

Her cabin'd, ample Spirit,
It flutter'd and fail'd for breath.
To-night it doth inherit
The vasty hall of Death.

Requiescat – Matthew Arnold

ZENOBIA

A TRAGEDY

So close and yet so far apart

You did not come in regal pomp
You did not come in splendour
You did not come on a snow-white charger
But only - as the company commander!

The Company Commander
by Sophia Z Kovachevich

My Name is Zenobia. I grew up with my brothers James and Joseph. But that was a long time ago. My brothers got married and they now have their families – children and grandchildren. We meet up - all the family a few times in the year. That is really very good for all of us to keep the family traditions alive.

Here I'd like to tell you my story.

I was born a long time ago. My brothers and I had great times together in spite of the occasional squabbling. They are good boys – my two brothers. We went to school and did all the things that people do that together make up our memories. And memories are good and bad, happy and sad; sombre and light-hearted. Some memories we treasure and remember and some we try to forget. But if you stop to think a moment – memories are a great gift. They are your lifelong companions and as we go along we keep adding to them.

Here I will share some of my memories with you.

One day, when I was five years old, I was walking and then I realised that I had climbed up a tree and could not get down. My maid while searching for me came under the tree and I told her I was stuck. She called the gardener who came with a ladder and got me down.

Maid and my governess together: *How did you get up there?*

Me: *I don't know. Maybe Dad's eagle flew me up there to show me how it looks like from up there.*

Maid & governess: *Why would the eagle do that?*

Me: *Because he likes me and flew me up on his back.*

Laughter from them

Another time someone shot at an owl in its wing and while I was walking in the garden it fell in our garden. I rushed in to tell dad and he told the man in charge of the birds to see to it. But before they could take the owl to the vet, I hugged it and told Owlie not to worry. The owl never hurt me at all. Later in the day I went to talk to my father's eagle as I did everyday and to visit sweet Owlie. Later I told my governess how smart Owlie was. I was teaching her to count and when I said two, she replied *twhoo*. So I decided to teach Owlie the alphabets also. Soon her wing healed and then Owlie flew away to her family. I missed her.

I loved all our animals and birds. I loved the horses too. The big horse would blow on my neck which made me laugh and laugh. I used to take carrots or apples for them.

Once when I was around six or seven at school our teacher asked us who each of us was named by and why. All my friends had regular names like Alice, Mary, Betty, Jo, Jenny, James, Alex etc. Then it was my turn. The teacher asked me why I had such an unusual name and if there was someone in my family or friends with the same name. I said I did not know but would ask my mother and report it to the class on Monday.

When I went home that day I followed my mother around until she told me why they had named me Zenobia. She said that once while watching a documentary they came across this name. It had belonged to a very strong and good Syrian Queen in Palmyra. I was very pleased and decided to try something out with the household and if it worked, I'd repeat it in school with more embellishments. I went through my mother's scarf drawers until I found a semi-transparent scarf. I then got a dress and a red, velvet sheet. Then I searched until I came up with a circlet for my head. I took out my favourite pair of red shoes. I also took a red lipstick from my mother's dressing table. I had to look authentic. Once I had got all that I wanted, I set to work. I put on the dress and some nice necklaces from my mother's jewellery box. Then I put on my shoes. I wasn't sure what to do with the scarf. I wasn't sure if it all had to go to the back of the head or if it was also supposed to cover my face. I settled to have the longer part at the back but enough to cover my face just a little. I tied the red sheet to act as a queen's robe. I put my mother's lipstick generously on and finally added the circlet made from Christmas decorations. I was ready to be a queen. For maximum effect I decided to parade around – everyone was bound to see me sooner or later. Before I had even made the first circle, my maid turned up and said:

Maid: *Miss what on earth are you doing?*

Me: *Do not address me as Miss. Address me as Your Majesty Queen Zenobia.*

Maid: *but why*

Me*: Because I am Queen Zenobia.*

The maid burst into laughter. I felt affronted but said nothing. I assumed, correctly, she had never heard of queen Zenobia. She left me but soon came back with other maids and workers including the chauffer. They all laughed. I told my maid: *You may carry my train and you others may follow me.* There was constant laughter from them. They did not understand that you are not supposed to laugh at Queen Zenobia, but I forgave them. Then more people joined in and the message was passed along: We are the followers of Queen Zenobia. There was a loud burst of laughter and a lot of snickering and trite comments. I ignored it all as it was beneath the queen to acknowledge such crass behaviour from her following. Finally I decided to call it a day and revert to simply Zenobia.

Next morning when I went to school, and when class was just about to begin, up went my hand.

Teacher: *Yes Zenobia, you have something to say?*

Zenobia: *Yes Miss Walters. I know something about my name Zenobia.*

The class started snickering: *she knows something about herself!*

Zenobia: *Don't be silly. It is about the other Zenobia.*

Teacher: *Okay Zenobia tell us.*

Zenobia: *she was a famous queen and fought many battles. She had something to do with Rome, a place called Paylr or something like that and some other countries.*

Teacher*: It's Palmyra I believe that you want. Thank you, Zenobia. You may sit down.*

The class was duly impressed.

But as children are, by the first break it was all forgotten.

Zenobia was very pleased with herself.

Then came summer and the family, as was usual, went to the seaside for a week. Zenobia loved the sea. She liked swimming but being young did not know her stamina. Her father's dog – a German Shepard always travelled with them. He usually accompanied Zenobia into the water.

One day after Zenobia had finished making her sand castle and driving everyone crazy with all her questions, her father suggested she go for a swim. Zenobia was very pleased and followed the dog – Rex into the water. No one noticed when she went in too deep and got into trouble. Rex noticed and picked her up by her clothes, brought her to where her parents were and dropped her soaking wet and out of breath at her parents feet.

Parents: *Zenobia, what's the matter with you?*

Zenobia: *I wondered if I could race Rex but the water wouldn't let me.*

Father: *Zenobia how many times have we told you not to swim alone in the sea but stay on the shore?*

Zenobia : *But dad, the mermaids were calling me to join them. I could not say no. I didn't want to say No. It was fun at the beginning but not after. Anyway Rex helped me so that's good. Come Rex I'll race you!*

Another time Zenobia saw her mother's pet peacock chasing a bird. So she decided to chase the peacock who really did not appreciate Zenobia's company. So instead of the bird he chased Zenobia. Zenobia gave up. Her maid who generally accompanied her everywhere laughed at the scene. Zenobia was not impressed and decided to find something else to amuse herself with. Face painting!

Still another time, she decided to miss her Maths class and instead climb a tree at school and wait to see when they would miss her. She also wanted to talk with the birds but none of them appreciated her company and they all flew away. Zenobia amused herself up there reciting poetry in her head. Unfortunately for her the headmistress of the school stood under the tree talking to the school gardener. Zenobia wanted to hide properly but unfortunately the thin branch of her new choice could not support her weight. Crash, the branch broke and Zenobia tumbled down in front of the headmistress' feet. Shock and consternation.

Headmistress : *Zenobia what on earth are you doing up a tree instead of being in class?*

Zenobia: *The birds called me.*

Headmistress: *Go wait in my office.*

Zenobia : *Yes, ma'am. But I can't walk.*

Zenobia's parents were called. She had broken her leg. That was the end of that adventure.

A FATEFUL MEETING

Years passed and life was good. Zenobia finished her GCE and then 'A' levels. Then while they were travelling in one of the countries, civil war broke out and they were stuck for a while. They sat it out until the army came to their rescue. They returned home. All foreigners who had been caught up in the civil war returned home safely.

At this time Zenobia was a very self-assured, pretty and charming young 15-year old. It was the early seventies and flower power was the motif all around. Love was the most important thing. Not war or killing or any such horrible things. *Love not war,* was one of the commonest slogans among the younger generation. *Flower Power* was another. Many tried drugs but not Zenobia.

The Vietnam War was finally over. The world sighed in relief. The downside was still not public knowledge. The young especially were on an emotional high. Drug experimentation was open and legal. But Zenobia was not into drugs at all. She had turned into a quite serious but charming young teen. She loved reading and travelling. She hadn't yet decided what to study at the university. She was on a break still.

Zenobia got on well with her brothers and she also had a lot of friends. They spent time not only philosophising but also fantasising about love and romance. Life was good. They discussed which department of the university they wanted to join. Some were going to study medicine, some history. Zenobia finally announced one day that she wanted to become a writer. So she wanted to study Literature. Moreover, if she studied literature she could enjoy her love of reading without guilt or wasting study time by frittering it away with books. Her parents thought that was a good idea. James had joined the army and Joseph had gone in for law. The children all seemed to be okay.

The University accepted Zenobia as her grades were very good. She was an excellent student. Zenobia was excited. She would be meeting new people, learning new things, going places. She loved university life.

On James' first holiday he came home with a friend. Zenobia fell in love totally and completely and most unexpectedly as she had a very strong feminist streak in her. He was a captain and was in charge of James' group. His name was Capt. Michael Alexander Kane. He preferred to be known by his middle name as Alexander or Alex. Zenobia was tongue-tied, perhaps for the first time in her adult life. All she did was stare at him when she thought he was not looking. She hardly ate anything. Somehow the evening passed in a haze for her.

Later that night James asked her why she didn't like his friend Alex. Zenobia did not reply directly. She said he seemed very nice. James hardly recognised this shy sister of his who had always had a retort for anything and everything. He asked her if she was sick. She said no. Zenobia herself did not understand her reaction so how could she explain it to James? She ended up by saying that she had a bit of a headache. James was satisfied and asked her to join him and Alex after dinner for a nightcap and a couple of games of card. She agreed.

They played a few hands and then they decided to talk. Alex wanted to know more about Zenobia. As usual, she got the same response to her name: *What an unusual name*! And Zenobia proudly explained adding that Queen Zenobia of Palmyra was related to Augustus Caesar and to Cleopatra. Alex was duly impressed and asked her how she knew so much about Queen Zenobia. She said that she had researched it. He asked her how she felt having such an unusual historic name. No one had ever asked her this question. Zenobia was very pleased indeed and replied that she was proud and honoured to have such a wonderful name and that she had decided to try and live up to it. One day she planned to write a book about Queen Zenobia because she had not found any books on her. There was information and cold hard facts. She intended to make Queen Zenobia come alive. Alex was really impressed and asked if she could send him a signed copy when it was completed. In fact, he suggested that she should begin work on it as soon as possible. She did not need a degree to write and James had told him that she was very good with words. Zenobia was in seventh heaven. He seemed to like her and seemed to be interested in her. James noticed how his sister glowed and made an excuse to let them talk for a while. And talk they did. They shared a common code of ethics, love of animals, love of nature and many other things Time passed very quickly. James returned and joined in their conversation. Soon it was time to go to bed. It was quite late. Zenobia said goodnight to both and left. She was very happy.

The next day Alex left to visit his family. James noticed a marked change in his sister. She had become much more subdued but there was a glow about her. She had always been happy but now she looked different. It was hard to pinpoint in what way. James decided to be blunt with her.

James: *Zenobia, don't be upset but I'd like to ask you something because I love you. You are my one and only baby sister. Would you mind?*

Zenobia: *No James, go ahead.*

James: *Zen, are you in love with Alex?*

Zenobia: *Yes. I think he is wonderful.*

James: *I suspected so. He is a very good person. You couldn't have chosen any one better.*

Zenobia: *James will you let me know how he's doing when you write to me or call? Do you think he likes me?*

James: *Sure sis. And as for your second question, it is extremely hard for anyone not to like you. But promise that you will go slowly and carefully and won't do anything silly that can have bad repercussions.*

Zenobia: *That's easy. I would never jeopardise my honour and that of my family but I'd like to spend the rest of my life as his wife. I am really in love with him.*

James knew his sister very well. They had always been very close. He was relieved. He knew she never made promises that she would not keep. James was glad he'd brought up this topic.

A couple of days later James went back to his unit. The house settled back into the old routine. But there was a difference. Everyone noticed, as James had earlier, that Zenobia was much more subdued but there was a glow about her. Her parents put it down to a good rest. Joseph was always busy with his studies or work and seldom participated in things around the house. He was the most introverted of the three children. But he spent more time around Zenobia than before. He must have noticed the change in her too. But he didn't comment on anything.

JAMES & ALEX

Before James' next leave, Alex had a serious conversation with James. He asked if he could have a talk with James' father and mother. James of course, was intrigued and wanted to know why.

Alex: *It's simple really though I must first explain to you the same question that I plan to ask your parents. Do you mind if I ask for your sister's hand in marriage? That's what I'm going to ask your parents. We can get engaged and when Zenobia finishes her university, we can get married. What do you think?*

James: *To tell the truth, I'm not surprised. And I'm sure she'll be very pleased. She's in love with you, you know. My parents, I'm sure will have no objections. In fact that will be a positive in your favour. Nowadays no one asks the parents. What made you think of that?*

Alex: *You seem like a very traditional family and I want everything to be as perfect as possible. Why don't we both take a couple of days leave and settle this soon?*

James: *Yes, that's a good idea.*

Alex: *I'll see to the leave right away.*

They applied and got leave and all was settled for the coming Thursday. James called and informed his family that he would be bringing Alex again. He called Zenobia separately and told her that Alex was coming mainly to see her. Zenobia was very happy. Maybe this is what was meant to be. On the other hand, it seemed too good to be true. She went to say a special thank you prayer.

Time hung heavily. The minutes dragged as did the hours and days. And finally it was Thursday. Zenobia got up very early and dressed very carefully in a cornflower blue dress that suited her very well. Then she waited. She wasn't hungry and so she skipped breakfast.

At university she could not concentrate on the lectures at all and realised it was really a waste of time. So she left and went home. She decided to miss the last two lectures so she'd be back home by lunchtime. It would give her time to prepare for her meeting with Alex.

Zenobia, the person who never went near the kitchen decided to try her hand at salad making. Everyone waited to see what she'd produce. This was totally out of character, but wonder of wonders it was quite good.

Finally, the boys came. Zenobia totally forgot her special salad. She rushed to her room to try and compose herself and wait for James to call her. She took out the paper written in beautiful script that she had written out for Alex from one of her favourite poets. She rolled it and tied it with a cornflower blue ribbon to match her dress. This is what was written:

Ah Love! Could thou and I with Fate
conspire
To grasp this sorry Scheme of things
Entire,
Would not we shatter it to bits — and
Then
Re-mould it nearer to the Heart's Desire !

Rubaiyat of Omar Khayyam *LXXIII*
Edward Fitzgerald

She had decided to give it to him before they left to go back to their barracks.

THE PROPOSAL

The visit began well as most visits do. Alex was given the spare bedroom like the time before. After washing up, they sat around making small talk altogether and having a before dinner glass. The only one who contributed nothing but sat tongue-tied was Zenobia. No one commented. Her behaviour in the recent past was anything but ordinary and almost everyone suspected the reason why, perhaps except her dad. He never noticed anything unless it was brought to his attention and no one had done so.

Dinner went off without a hitch. The food, all commented, was excellent. The cook had outdone himself. Zenobia hardly touched her food. When her mother and Alex both remarked on it, she said she wasn't hungry.

After dinner James told his father that Alex wanted to speak to Dad and Mum. Mum suspected why. Dad asked James to come in with them. After all, Alex was James' friend and had the right to be privy to whatever it was that Alex wanted to say. Of course James knew the score. So they all went into the small living room except for Zenobia.

There, as James reported to Zenobia later, Alex formally asked for permission to propose to Zenobia.

Zenobia's parents asked if it wasn't too early and Alex said no. He had never been seriously involved with anyone else and had never wanted to either. Zenobia was the only girl for him. Permission was gladly given on condition that they would wait until after Zenobia's 18th birthday to get married. And then Alex was told that he could go and speak to Zenobia himself. Alex got up with alacrity and went in search of Zenobia. She was sitting in the lounge wondering how the talk was progressing. Alex asked her to walk a bit with him and they went into the garden. Alex proposed.

Zenobia accepted. Both were very happy. They complemented each other perfectly and made a lovely couple. Alex had come prepared with a ring. Zenobia dragged Alex back into the house and announced to all her news. Her father ordered champagne and everyone toasted the couple. They decided to wait until Zenobia finished her university – which would be in two and a half years. Her parents thought it was a very good idea as they would get to know each other better and not rush into marriage. Zenobia wanted to get married immediately but agreed to wait. Alex's parents rang to congratulate the couple. Zenobia's parents invited them for a visit and to get to know each other. A date was set for their first face-to-face meeting and all was well.

This visit passed off as in a dream. After James and Alex went back to the barracks, Alex and Zenobia exchanged letters every day.

Alex's parents took to Zenobia - it was nothing unusual. People generally liked her. She had a way of charming all who she met. They, again as usual, asked her about her name and she told them. They too were suitably impressed. Zenobia's life seemed to be moving on oiled wheels. Everything was just right.

Whenever possible, Alex visited Zenobia. Sometimes they went to the cinema or the zoo but mostly they stayed home, listened to music and danced. Joseph when informed was also very happy for his little sister. On one of Alex's visit, Joseph came down to see them and welcome Alex into the family. He too, liked Alex. It really was like a story book romance but don't you just know when things are very good, something is bound to go wrong!

Alex was posted to Ireland and Zenobia freaked out. There was a lot of unrest at that time especially with the Sinn Fein. Alex wrote everyday but Zenobia didn't always get the letters on time. Still the time passed and Alex's term there was over and he was back. He got leave and came to see Zenobia and the family. Zenobia was ecstatic. It was a lovely reunion. They set a date for the wedding. Both wanted a spring wedding – just four months away. They wanted a rather small wedding – just the two families and some close friends - about 50 guests in all.

The formal engagement was to be in three weeks' time followed by the wedding. The following days and weeks were spent in looking at designs for the formal engagement party, the engagement and wedding dress and accessories for both and so on. Time simply flew by.

Alex called Zenobia as often as he could. Life was beautiful. They were very happy.

A month later, they had the engagement party. Zenobia looked simply beautiful. They made a very good-looking couple. Everyone was happy for Zenobia, especially her family, relatives and friends.

Alex was again posted to Northern Ireland but only for a short time, they said. The time dragged and then one day Zenobia received a wire from his regiment saying that Alex had died in the line of duty. A sniper bullet got him on his way back to the base.

Zenobia was shattered. She changed overnight, so-to-speak. She no longer laughed. She lost her *joie de vivre*. She withdrew to a place where none could follow her.

It took her a long, long time to get back a modicum of adjustment. Her grief was palpable.

Zenobia never married or wrote anything but devoted her whole life to helping others. She withdrew into herself and no-one, not even James, her favourite brother could reach her. She was dry-eyed but never laughed again. She became an emotional recluse.

By her bedside she kept these framed words:

No more let life divide
What death can join together!

Adonais – P.B. Shelley

Then at the age of 40, she died peacefully in her sleep. They said she died of a broken heart. She faded into death. She was reunited with her beloved in the land where there is no pain or sorrow. God rest both their souls in peace.

COUSIN DAVID

Turning and turning in the widening gyre
The falcon cannot see the falconer:
Things fall apart; the centre cannot hold;
Mere anarchy is loosed upon the world,
The blood-dimmed tide is loosed and everywhere
The ceremony of innocence is drowned;

The Second Coming by W B Yeats

COUSIN DAVID

David was a cousin of ours. I remember him rather vaguely as he was killed when I was around seven or eight years old. His death showed me the ephemerality of life and that one should make the most of the good times whenever you can. I suppose, in hindsight that it was a tragedy waiting to happen.

David was much older than us. He was married and had three daughters. The youngest was the same age as I was. He did not work at any regular job as he had family income but he loved flying his helicopter. Sometimes he used to take his assistant along with him when he wanted to take aerial photographs. He was a fun person and we all loved him. He gave us lots of piggyback rides.

I went up in his copter a few times. The world just looks different from up in the air and adrenalin courses through your veins. It is a feeling of danger, excitement and adventure. My parents trusted him enough to let me go up in the air with him. My siblings weren't impressed. I think they were afraid.

David and his family often visited us. We got along like a house on fire with his girls. I don't remember his wife clearly. She was a quiet person but very nice to us. She used to have fun toys for us to play with and lots of ice-cream.

David was very tall. He looked like a giant to us and heavy built. I remember when he sat us on his shoulder and took us for a walk. The ground looked very far away. It was exciting. It felt dangerous. I loved it!

Our dogs also liked all of them. When they visited us or we visited them there was always a lot of noise and excitement. But such is life that everything ends. I suppose in any case we would have lost contact as time passed as they were planning to move to Canada.

One morning David came to visit us and we children were banished from being with the adults as he wanted to talk seriously with my parents. In hindsight I think he must have had a premonition.

David: *Kids I'll see you in a little while and I can take you up for a spin.*

My siblings all together: *Oh no. You can give us piggy rides and take us out in the car for ice cream.*

Me: *I'll go for a spin. You didn't take me with you for many days now.*

David: *Okay kids. Now you go and play. I'll see you in a short while.*

David to our parents: *I need to talk to you about some important matters and ask for your advice and help.*

Our parents: *Let's go to the library. It's better than the drawing room, if you want privacy. Otherwise we can talk here.*

I was as quiet as a mouse because this sounded exciting. I wanted to know what the matter was. I liked David and wanted to help him too. I was even ready to lend him my favourite toy dog, Jaspar to keep him company.

David: *Let's go to the library. I don't want the kids to overhear what I want to talk with you about.*

I was even more intrigued as all children are wont to be if an adventure is in the wings. I decided to hide in the library and hear what they wanted to talk in secret about. It seemed like a great adventure. It reminded me about the time I hid in a cupboard to see how long before someone missed me and came looking for me. That was not very entertaining at all. The cupboard door self-locked and I was unable to open it from the inside or even to be heard. Finally to my relief my banging on the door and screaming was finally heard and I was let out. So this time I had no intention of locking myself anywhere but hiding under the table. Life was fun!

I rushed to the library and hid under the farthest table so when they sat down no one would know I was there but I could hear clearly. I have always had acute hearing skills. Now the stage was set. All I had to do was - wait. I recited poetry in my head while I waited. I loved and still love poetry. Actually what I loved as a child I still do so. Nothing had changed concerning that.

After what seemed like years, my parents and David and Alice came into the library and sat down at one of the reading tables.

David: *Uncle and Aunt I'm really grateful for your support.*

My Dad: *That's okay David. Now what's going on?*

Davis: *I'd like to make you and aunt as the executors of my Will.*

My mum: *Why David? You're only 32 years old. You have your whole life ahead of you. What's the hurry?*

David: *I have my reasons. Tomorrow I'll come over and ask your personal assistants – yours Uncle and yours Aunt to be witnesses, if you don't mind. Alice and I discussed it and we both feel it's something that has to be done - the sooner, the better. And there's no better people than you that we feel we can count on.*

My Mum: *But David, you haven't yet answered my question. Why? At least give us a reason.*

David: *For one thing we might move to Canada but the main reason is that I will start flying helicopters for a living and I want to know that my family will have support – should anything happen to me.*

My Mum: *Of course you can depend on us. But I'll talk in more detail to you tomorrow.*

David and Alice: *Thanks. We'll come over around the same time tomorrow and I hope I can answer most of your questions and put your minds at ease.*

I waited until they left and went to tell my siblings all what I had learned. It was a big secret. But why? What's a will? What is ex ex... whatever? Why do the personal assistants need to wit – whatever? What is that? So many questions and no answers! The only thing I learned was that David, Aunt Alice and the kids would go faraway and David would fly a lot – without me. No more piggyback rides or ice cream with the girls. Boring!!!

None of us understood the ramifications of making out a Will. We didn't even know what a Will was or why it was such a hush-hush affair. But it seemed to be an exciting secret. We decided that I'd hide in the library again. Anyway it was one of my favourite places. I have always loved books – the smell of them, the feel of them and their contents. I've always read from the time I learned to read. And of course to look at all the gorgeous children's books' illustrations! My parents had a bookshelf there for our books too even though we had our personal bookshelves upstairs in the children's playroom. I preferred the big library. It somehow felt different there. One felt at peace, safe and happy. My love of books is still with me.

And as children will, after a short time we all forgot about it as we continued with our usual pursuits. Our governesses suggested that we children prepare a play for our parents' anniversary two months later. We were very excited and decided to rope in Georgina, Jacky and Emily – our nieces – David's kids. It was funny being an aunt to someone older than you – me younger and Georgina older. We were more like siblings than anything else because they visited us every weekend and we got along very nicely. But later on, we lost touch when they were in their late teens and Georgina was 22. She fell in love and moved to Spain.

But I digress. As I was saying I went to the library and waited. In a short while they came.

David: *Once again thank you for your understanding. You see I have to make sure the girls and Alice will be alright should something happen to me.*

My Mum: *What could happen? You are young and in excellent health.*

David: *Yes, I know that but we have no one in Canada and I'd just like to make sure everything goes smoothly and they are taken care of. It's one less worry for me.*

My dad: *Well, let's see the papers and forms. Have you had them checked over by a lawyer?*

David: *Yes, this morning by the family lawyer.*

My dad: *Okay then.*

My parents signed and then rang for their personal assistants to come in and witness the documents.

By this time I was bored and fell asleep on the carpet under the table waiting for them to leave. I suddenly woke up as it was not as comfortable as my bed. There was no one in the library except me. I went upstairs.

My siblings: Why has it taken you so long and what is the matter?

Me: It was all very boring. They signed papers.

Soon we forgot all about this. Life continued much as usual. We saw Cousin David, Alice and the kids regularly.

Our parents wedding anniversary was on the 29th of December, between Christmas and New Year. We prepared for the show. Georgina, Jacky and Emily all had their part to play.

Christmas came and our gifts. We all got what we wanted. It was smashing! We had a family Christmas as we did each year.

New Year was less fun as we were allowed to stay up until five minutes past twelve.

So far, everything was fine. My sister had her birthday on January 2nd and we had another party – for us children. Then came cold, cold February. I hated February for a long time after that year. It was a blood-red day of woe.

It was on A Sunday and David had promised to take me for a spin in his helicopter. None of my siblings or his girls liked going up in the chopper. But I loved it. It was so exhilarating. I loved the speed and the danger.

David called and cancelled for Sunday but said we could go up on Monday. I was happy and on Monday we went for a spin. Little did I know then that it would be my last trip with Cousin David.

Wednesday morning my mum came up to our room as we were studying. She informed us that Cousin David was dead. His chopper had had an accident.

We were not allowed to go to the funeral. Years later I learnt why. Part of his head was cut off.

I have never gone up in another helicopter. And I won't ever either.

David's premonition came true. He was a very good person

We missed him for a long time. My parents took even more care of his family. It hit all of us really hard. His family moved in with us in another part of the house because they wanted to. But as time passed we went our different ways. They do keep in touch with my parents. Not as much with me because I took to travelling a lot.

Alice remarried when Emily, the youngest was 16 years old. The girls continued to stay with my parents until they finished their education and got jobs.

We loved David. He was a large part of our lives. We all missed him. He was a happy and fun person. No one can ever take his place in our hearts. We often talked about him. Not much now. Time passes and other things intervene. Now we are all of us married with other responsibilities. Time moves on and the pain dulls but I think none of us will ever forget him and his kindness and love towards us.

May his soul rest in peace forever and forever AMEN!

SELENA

PROLOGUE

My name is Karen. Selena and I have known each other all our lives. Like Selena, I too, am an only child. Our parents were friends and we grew up together. In fact we generally thought of ourselves as sisters. We played together, schooled together, went to High school together and the university. We trusted each other fully.

Selena was one of the nicest, gentlest spirits that I have ever known. She was very sensitive and so got hurt very easily. However there was a tensile strength about her. In all the time I knew her, she forgave everyone except for one person whose betrayal really cut her to the quick.

It is now up to me to tell you Selena's story

With rue my heart is laden
  For golden friends I had
For many a rose-lipt maiden
  And many a lightfoot lad

By brooks too broad for leaping
  The lightfoot lads are laid
The rose-lipt maids are sleeping
  In fields where roses fade

A Shropshire Lad by A.E.Housman

CHAPTER 1

Selena was a very interesting and unusual girl. She was appropriately named for the moon and showed the moon's characteristics of beauty and emotionality. She was a happy, healthy curious person who always found something interesting in the world around her. Being the apple of her parents' eye she always got what she wanted. And being very sweet-natured, it was hard to deny her anything. But she had a lot of compassion and kindness in her. All who knew her doted on her. Being the only grandchild her grandparents doted on her too.

Selena took risks in her love for adventure that others would have thought many times before doing so. Selena was fun to be with even though she had a very serious side to her too. She loved music especially Mozart. She also loved modern music – the Carpenters, Elvis Presley, Cliff Richard, Simon and Garfunkle, Carol Bayer Sager, Lionel Richie etc. But she loved reading most of all followed by her love of animals. She was an accomplished horse rider. All the animals – and there were many – loved her. I suppose they sensed her innate kindness and gentleness.

Often Selena and her friends went to the Disco but they were not permitted to stay out after 11pm.

At school she did extremely well and after her A Levels she decided to study Political Science for her Bachelor's degree and continue with that for her Master's Degree. Everyone was surprised at her choice as she had not shown any particular leaning towards Politics.

Selena finished her Bachelors with flying colours and went onto her Master's Degree.

CHAPTER 2

At the university in her free time, she decided to study French in the evening with some of her friends. At that class in a short while she became friends with a young man named Anthony who had fallen in love with her - head-over heels. Selena wasn't impressed but she liked him and they often went to discoes as a group with some other friends.

One unfortunate day, Anthony introduced her to a friend of his – Horace. Horace was studying medicine at the same University but in another building. He wanted to become a gynaecologist. He became obsessed with wanting Selena as his girlfriend. Truth to tell, she too, was attracted to him. So they got together. Anthony was heartbroken. But what can one do? Love takes as it pleases with no apology to the victims or the bystanders.

Horace and Selena became an item in their groups. It came as a shock to many because Selena was a well-known women's rights person. This was one time they saw her dating and often being unsure of herself. She introduced him to her family and they took him under their wings as he was a foreign student there. Everyone thought that he was a serious, honest and good man. He was a bit older than Selena. But Selena didn't care. This was a new kind of adventure. Her mother tried to warn her to be careful but who can advise first love or even more, young love???

Selena was shocked at her own weakness. What on earth was going on? This is NOT how she had planned out her life. There was to be no male dominance or interference in her life. She was balking. So Horace proposed and after some deep thinking Selena accepted. They became an engaged couple going everywhere together. Selena's family all loved him and thought that he would be good for Selena. He was very pragmatic. He was also his mother's favourite child. They were to marry after he finished his studies. Selena and her family were to either have the wedding at her place (more likely) or go over to his place. He was an American from Houston, Texas.

Time flew by. They went everywhere together. He had no sisters only two younger brother. They came over to study in England too and met and liked Selena, especially his youngest brother, Cody.

Horace finished his degree and went home to his parents in Texas. At first the letters and calls came regularly and then slowly they diminished and finally there was silence. Selena thought that perhaps he was unwell or maybe the new job was too onerous for him to have much free time. So she asked his brothers. They were surprised that she did not know what was going on. He was married to a girl of his mother's choosing. Selena had no words and cut him out of her life completely and totally. She felt terribly betrayed.

She would never ever forgive this betrayal – after 5 years together. Meanwhile being the person she was she did not have a broken heart but a badly bruised ego. She decided to cut her losses. But why did he not tell her? This really troubled her. He could have said he had fallen in love with someone else and it would all have been okay. Why simply disappear, not reply to letters or phone calls and leave it to his siblings to tell her? Why? Oh why this type of lie and subterfuge? Was this his plan from the start? - To use her, her family and contacts and then disappear? Was it just expediency? Probably. It didn't matter because what goes around, comes around- sooner or later.

CHAPTER 3

Selena had finished her studies and was working as a lecturer in Politics at a College. She put all her energy into that. And she did extremely well. She was a favourite with the other faculty members. They loved her positive and vibrant spirit.

Now Horace's family lived in Houston, Texas and his brothers came over to England for a working visit. They often visited her. Once they came with their cousin, Malcolm. It was instantaneous attraction between the two. He was as unlike Horace as chalk is from cheese. His name was Malcolm. He was fun-loving open, agreeable and as adventurous as Selena was.

Selena was young – only 24 years old. She was from a rather well-off family with not a lot of exposure to the harsh side of life. Malcolm was truly head-over heels in love with her. – a reciprocal love, I must say. They decided to get together and Malcolm moved to England, got a job with an engineering firm and the two decided to pair up. Neither at this point thought of settling down. They wanted to get to know each other while both having their own places. Time would tell where this would go. Malcolm took her to his home and introduced her to all his family – parents, siblings and even Horace's mother, his maternal aunt, as a very important person in their lives. That was something!

So the years passed and Malcolm became more and more possessive. Selena wanted to be free. She could not handle this type of possessiveness as they were not formally engaged. They were just accepted everywhere as a couple. He took her to visit his sisters in Houston to their houses and they loved her especially his favourite sister. It was a catch 22. The more jealous Malcolm became, the more Selena pushed back and that made him wilder. The simple solution was for them to tie the knot. But there was a big problem here. Horace and Malcolm were first cousins. Their mothers were sisters and they were a very close knit family. In the long run it might lead to bad blood between them. As it was the two cousins had stopped talking to each other and rarely saw each other.

Selena, being an only child wasn't mature enough to see this but her mother did and advised caution. She had already been engaged to Horace for a number of years. That could not be wiped away and it was bound to have repercussions if Selena now married Malcolm. Horace meanwhile had tried, very unsuccessfully, to meet up with Selena again. She did not give him the time of day. There was nothing to say about his betrayal and cowardice. She could not forgive that. And if once he had behaved so shamefully what was there to stop him doing the same or worse again? No it would not do. He was out of her life and she meant to keep it that way.

Selena had told Malcolm about Horace's overtures and that made Malcolm fume and fret. It was better he heard it from her than from his cousin or cousins.

Unfortunately the conversation became a huge argument. Neither could see the other's point of view. Malcolm because he was jealous and Selena because she thought she was being more than fair in informing Malcolm. He was supposed to be appreciative – not jealous. Malcolm left in a temper.

CHAPTER 4

At about midnight Malcolm called to apologise. Selena was happy again. Malcolm too was happy. They decided to have a serious chat. They settled to go out for dinner then return to Selena's flat and have a serious talk and clear the air on the next day.

Next day was a Saturday. It was a beautiful spring morning. The heart feels lighter on such days and problems seem inconsequential. They met up and everything was resolved. Apologies were made and accepted. Life was good again. Things went back to as they were – more or less. Malcolm and Selena went everywhere together. They looked very much in love. But there was a niggling in Selena's heart. Where was this leading to? Nothing seemed to be happening and time was passing. But she did not bring up the topic with Malcolm - why? She once said to me that she was tired of living in limbo. Malcolm should either marry her or let her go. She would accept either solution if it made him happy. She really loved Malcolm – genuinely.

A week later, Malcolm's mother prepared a nice picnic lunch for them and the two had a wonderful time together. The weather was perfect and they enjoyed the fresh air almost as much as each other's company. It was a dreamtime when all problems and negative thoughts were left behind. They spent the whole day, enjoying the fresh air and swimming in the nearby lake. It was simply a perfect day!

At the end of the day, Malcolm dropped her off at her flat promising to be back shortly. Selena was happy. She thought that they had made progress and maybe tonight would be the night he proposed.

Malcolm came and they had a nice dinner prepared by Selena who was a very good cook. They only talked inanities. Selena waited patiently for a topic that never came. At the end of the evening, Malcolm went home. Nothing serious was discussed. Selena was very disappointed.

But we have to consider Malcolm's plight. It wasn't easy for him either.

But the problem was that Malcolm was obsessed with her. He could not marry her or leave her. He was in a quandary. She was all he wanted but it was not possible. His family all loved Selena but they knew it would lead to problems later, down the track. Every time there was a family gathering or Selena and Horace met or saw each other it would lead to an argument or fight. They had seen it happen already. Malcolm could not deal with Selena having been Horace's fiancée before - even now.

And an even greater problem was that she did not bring up the topic with Malcolm. She discussed with me and I could not help her. What could I say? I did advise her to talk openly with Malcolm but she was not ready to do so. I think she was afraid of what he might say or do.

They continued in the same way for a couple of years more. Selena started to show severe depression which those who knew her well recognised. Finally Malcolm spoke to me and told me about his predicament. I did not advise him. It was not my place to do so but I did strongly suggest that he spoke openly with Selena.

A week later Selena's maid called me. She was frantic. Selena had tried to drown herself. I immediately went over to her place and gave her a sharp talking to. I said no one and absolutely no one was worth her life. She was young, pretty and healthy. And there were many other fish in the sea. She should put Malcolm aside and concentrate on herself and what made her contented – not necessarily happy. She simply listened but made no comment. She kissed me and said I was her sister in spirit.

Things more or less went back to normal – apparently. But I sensed a change in her. She no longer laughed whole-heartedly.

KAREN

A few months passed by and life went back to what it was. But I just could not shake off the feeling that somehow Selena had changed. There was nothing to show that she did but my unease persisted.

At first I thought perhaps it had something to do with Horace and his betrayal. After all he had proven himself. He was morally and physically bankrupt. He betrayed and contaminated anything he touched. It was a judgement on him that no matter how hard he tried, he could not procreate. That was his physically being bankrupt. We always pay for our sins – in one way or another.

Meanwhile, Selena was heartbroken. Selena did not want to go on. So she slipped into the land from where no one ever returns. She willed herself there and succeeded fading away before or eyes.

Selena descended into a depression. She rarely laughed or even smiled wholeheartedly. She lost her joie de vivre and started losing weight. She looked pale, wan and withdrawn. On an autumn day she suffered a major heart attack at the age of 38.

So passed away a wonderful soul. I think she died of a broken heart. The world will never be the same again.

> *They say she died of a broken heart*
> *I tell the tale as 'twas told to me*
> *But her spirit lives*
> *And her soul is part*
> *Of this sad old house by the sea*
> **Anonymous**

AMELIA

I am a part of all that I have met;
Yet all experience is an arch wherethro'
Gleams that untravell'd world, whose margin fades
For ever and for ever when I move

The Princess by Lord A. Tennyson

My name is Amelia. I will begin this story with my birth - as it was told to me. It seems like an aeon ago.

I was born in March 1955 to a very well-off family. But sad to say (it's good I'm still here to tell my story which is a weird one), when I was born, I looked dead. Of course in those far-off days technology was not so advanced and people were much more religious – especially my family. They accepted the fact that some babies are born dead. My baby coffin was ordered but it seems I had no intention of remaining dead. As the hearse drew into the driveway, I started howling to the top capacity of my little lungs. The hearse was sent away and I was fed and looked after. But that was not the last of my baby adventures. I tell the stories as they were told to me.

I was often found talking to the empty space – my invisible friends. Till today I have no idea what that was all about! It seems I always had an over-active imagination. I used to describe my invisible little friends in detail. Perhaps I was lonely and so created friends. Any way, they all said that I was advanced for my age. Once when I was a child, somehow I managed to get up a tree and then claimed that I was flown up there by an eagle to see the world from his point of view. That's imagination for you!

I was a very naughty child and often got into mischief – good mischief. Once I went to the kitchen, where we kids were not allowed to venture into and tried to jump over a pot of hot milk. I burnt my legs and the boots had to be cut and removed. It took a long while to heal and I was carried everywhere as my feet too were burnt though less than the legs. I still have those scars on my legs.

Another time I wanted to go out and play instead of doing my studies. I was home schooled by my governess and only later on I went to sit for the governmental exams. So I went out into the garden and decided to climb a tree which I did. Unfortunately for me my father had to choose my tree to stand under while talking to someone. I was nervous that if he looked up he would see me and both I and my governess would be in deep trouble. My parents were very strict. I gingerly tried to climb further up and hide behind the leaves but as luck would have it, the branch I was on gave way. Down I came from my perch, right at my father's feet. But I did not get into trouble that time as I had broken my leg and that was a reprieve. It seems that I had preferred a broken leg to my father's wrath.

Then there was the incident when I climbed up a post, lost my grip and fell on a nail. The doctor was called and I was extracted from the nail and had stitches performed on my head. Unfortunately for me they shaved off all my lovely hair. A month or so after this incident I was sliding down the bannister, and somehow came tumbling down instead of just slipping off the bannister. The stiches had to be redone. The scars are there on my head till today for anyone to see. Somehow, I always managed to get into hot water.

My childhood is scattered with memories both good and bad as everyone's is. But I believe in general, I had a very good childhood. And a lot of memories! I have always loved the colour red. When I was young my best present was a walking talking doll, the same height as I was, dressed in a green pinafore and the beautiful red shoes I got. I loved that pair of shoes and wore it all the time.

Of the myriad of countries I visited as a child, I remember some more than others. I remember living in the then country of Czechoslovakia. I loved my time there. I had a group of Czech friends and we spent a lot of our times together. I also remember the gypsy woman we saw in Rumania who once told me that I would die very far from the country I was born in and that I would marry late. That was in Rumania when I had just entered my teens. I did marry rather late. More of that later.

I also remember visiting China. I found the Chinese to be very nice people and very honest. Once I discarded a brand-new pair of socks but that pair followed me from one city to another.

When I was around ten years of age we went to the United States as my parents, who were avid travellers, wanted to go to California. So there we went! I was quite unhappy there. Everything was new and overpowering.

The buildings were very tall, there were too many cars on the road, people were very nice but very different.

I came from a very well-off family as I mentioned before. We had everything that we desired and more. But that bored me. I wanted something different. I wanted the life that others had. So I gave up my very cushioned life and decided to explore the world. True I had the support of my family to fall back on but I decided to cut loose. So I decided to travel as far away and as distant from my family as I could. I went to Africa because my family had nothing to do with that continent. In fact they didn't even know where I was going until the last possible moment. It was great. I learned a lot about life and how people were good and decent everywhere. You just needed to be yourself and accept people as they were. I travelled over to many North African countries and always met with acceptance and kindness. I have no bad memories of the time I spent there.

Then I decided to go to the Middle East as I had a number of friends there. I travelled through a wide swathe of the Middle East. It was so good that I stayed there for a long time. At one point I even thought I'd settle there but changed my mind as I felt I could not really adjust to their way of life – not because it was bad but because it was too different.

I also travelled widely throughout Europe and parts of Asia. Again, there were many good lessons to learn and many good memories to add to my cache of good memories. I guess I was lucky to see and experience the good rather than the bad in people around the world. That was an education in itself and it made me become the person I am.

I am a strong believer in women's equality and promoted that wherever I went. I believe women are as capable, if not more so in some instances, than men and they should have the same rights and opportunities as the men. I admire the suffragettes and all what they achieved. It upsets me to see how democratic USA is aiming to nullify the abortion bill. It is not for the men and a few misguided or brain-washed women to decide for us. We are very capable of charting our course in life. When all is said and done it is our body and how we treat it and what we ask of it should be our choice.

I have also always been an animal lover. I especially love dogs, cats, horses and hamsters. But I love other animals too. My future plan, once upon a time, was to buy a house on a large piece of land and adopt homeless dogs and have them cared for. But that did not happen. Instead I travelled.

During my travels I met someone and fell madly, totally in love with him. Soon after we got married and I must say I have been very happy with my choice and my life. Now about my one and only love: he really is a very special person and we suit each other perfectly. We have similar values and attitudes, similar likes and dislikes – in short, we are two halves of one whole.

Death is a long way away but when I die, I hope to wander in the new land and soak up new experiences, meet new entities, learn more about the universe and its inhabitants in a new ambience. Oh it's all so exciting!!– I want to wake up in a new place and begin a new life – the life after death. Death I think is an exciting, new journey to some place, some ambience, some part of the universe which we should embrace and welcome rather than fear because as Lord A. Tennyson said in **The Princess**:

> *Our echoes roll from soul to soul*
> *And grow forever and forever.*

How much more positive can the other world be? We leave our footsteps here and make fresh ones there. None disappear but they are put in the crucible of existence. I want to wake up dead and partake of all those new experiences that are awaiting me.

THE EPILOGUE

The one remains, the many change and pass,
Heaven's light forever shines, Earth's shadows fly;
*Life, like a dome of **many**-coloured glass,*
Stains the white radiance of Eternity,
Until Death tramples it to fragments...

Adonais - by PB Shelley

So ends these eight stories. Each has something to teach us. And even though death divided them all except one, they had moments, hours, days of bliss and pure love, love - which conquers death. It is better to live a short, happy fulfilled life than a long dreary one.

In the final analysis these stories are not about death and the loss of hope but of hope itself. Our lives are simply a transition from one state of being to another one.

I also posit to you about dreams. And premonitions. Why do we sometimes have dreams and premonitions that come true? True sometimes only in minor details – dreams and premonitions that become a reality. What gives us this view into the future? If life and existence ends once we die how to account for *déjà vu* and why do the dead come back in our dreams in the short and long future times? Why and how do they give us insights to what is yet to come true? Death is not the end of life but the beginning of another state of being, of another state of existence, I believe. Our material and physical bodies die and disintegrate but our souls – our spirits endure and go on to another plane of existence – of being. That is a major reason why this book is called WAKE UP DEAD– we wake up from a kind of sleep which is our manifestation of life in this world. When we wake up in the next world it is only one form of death that occurs here on earth to another existence.

I'll end with Wordsworth's famous lines from his ode *Intimations of Immortality* which encapsulates my view of death here:

a sleep and a forgetting:

And so we'll forget this world for the most part in the next and so it will continue. Death is only the end of one life and the beginning of another. It is simply a gateway to another world.

Printed in the United States
By Bookmasters